Around the Shores of Lake Erie

A Guide to Small Towns, Rural Areas and Natural Attractions

by

Donna Marchetti

GLOVEBOX
GUIDEBOOKS
OF AMERICA
1112 Washburn Place East
Saginaw, MI 48602-2977

Cover design by Dan Jacalone
Cover and all interior photos by Donna Marchetti
Editor, Penny Weber

Published by: **Glovebox Guidebooks of America**
1112 Washburn Place East
Saginaw, Michigan 48602-2977
(800) 289-4843 or (517) 792-8363

Library of Congress, CIP

Donna Marchetti, 1953-

Around the Shores of Lake Erie
(A Glovebox Guidebooks of America publication)

ISBN 1-881139-22-0

Printed in the United State of America

10 9 8 7 6 5 4 3 2 1

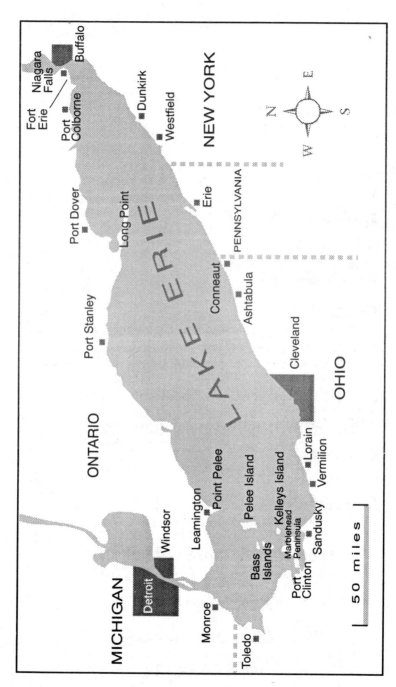

MICHIGAN

Detroit

Monroe

Toledo

Windsor

Leamington

Point Pelee

ONTARIO

Port Stanley

Port Dover

Port Colborne

Fort Erie

Niagara Falls

Buffalo

Dunkirk

Westfield

NEW YORK

Long Point

LAKE ERIE

Erie

PENNSYLVANIA

Conneaut

Ashtabula

Cleveland

OHIO

Bass Islands

Pelee Island

Kelleys Island

Marblehead Peninsula

Port Clinton

Sandusky

Lorain

Vermilion

N E S W

50 miles

Contents

Foreword

When I was a kid growing up in Cincinnati, I loved Lake Erie. I thought it was the ocean, and it may well have been for me, since it was the only large body of water I had ever seen.

Every summer our family would pile into the car and drive four hours north to a cottage on a sandy beach for two weeks filled with blue water and blazing sunsets. I remember waking up to watch the dawn over the lake, long strolls on the beach and wincing at the sharp clam shells beneath my feet while walking out over the sand bars. I loved the small towns around the area — Sandusky, Port Clinton, Marblehead — and the islands we'd venture out to occasionally.

But as an adult, I rarely visited the lake — even though I found myself living in Cleveland, only a few miles from its shore. Then I became curious. Was there still charm and beauty to be found on Lake Erie? In the summer of 1996 I decided to find out. My husband and I loaded up our bicycles with clothes and maps and set out from our home in Cleveland headed east, for a 755-mile ride all the way around the lake.

I was looking for the small towns, the beaches, the vineyards and rolling countryside most people don't even know exist. "What's on the other side?" Americans asked of the Canadian shore. Likewise, the Canadians, though likely to be familiar with Cleveland, Buffalo and Detroit, didn't seem to know much about the rest of the American side.

And there's plenty to know. We passed dozens of nature preserves, parks and wildlife areas; visited countless museums and historical sites; wandered the streets of peaceful lakeside ports and sampled the fruits of the region — crisp wines, the freshest of produce and lake-harvested perch and walleye. We found charming bed and breakfasts and a surprising number of memorable eating spots.

But we had to search for them. While planning our trip, we found plenty of information about the big cities on the lake, but frustratingly little when it came to the small towns and rural areas. We simply learned as we traveled. So, as often is the case for writers, the frustration spawned a book — the one I wish I'd had tucked into my bike pack when we left on that journey.

There have been many people, too numerous to list, who have provided information and suggestions vital to this guide. Among them were museum staff, representatives from chambers of commerce, bed and breakfast owners, and park officials to whom I am indebted for their assistance. I am also grateful to Glovebox Guidebooks for taking on this project. My greatest share of gratitude, however, must go to my husband Tony and my son Justin, who have been endlessly supportive, patient and helpful throughout the many months of travel, research and writing that went into this book.

Donna Marchetti

Introduction

Lake Erie is the oldest, shallowest, warmest and meanest of the Great Lakes. With an average depth of only 62 feet, it can whip itself into a fury in a matter of minutes. More than 500 ships rest on its bottom. From the late 1600s, when the first European schooner went below the waves, to the present day, captains have been forced to regard the lake with a cautious and respectful eye. When storms arise suddenly — as they often do — waves a car-length high can reduce a boat to a pile of splinters.

Fortunately, it's a gentler side of Lake Erie that we most often see: placid water, quiet waves and sunsets streaked across a wide-open sky. Around its shores, away from the cities, are scenes of beauty — a great blue heron pausing at a shoreline marsh, the wide expanse of a sandy beach, a vineyard carpeting a high-rising bluff — all framed by deep blue water of a clarity that would have seemed impossible only a few years ago.

Lake Erie was once the dirtiest of the Great Lakes. For years, waste from Cleveland, Detroit and Toledo was dumped unchecked into the lake until, by the 1970s, it was declared "dead." But because the lake is so shallow, the time it takes it renew itself, if allowed to, is relatively short. Though much of the improved water clarity is due to the filtering action of the zebra mussel, which arrived in the bilge water of foreign ships in the 1980s, the lake is far cleaner today than it was 20 years ago. While still in need of constant vigilance, it has made a remarkable recovery. There is plenty alive beneath its surface, including more than 100 species of fish, making it an important center for sport and commercial fishing. More fish from Lake Erie end up on people's plates than from all the other Great Lakes combined.

Lake Erie was the last of the Great Lakes to be discovered by Europeans. French explorer Louis Jolliet was the first to record seeing it in 1669. In 1679, the French ship Griffon set sail from the Niagara River to become the first European ship to traverse the length of the lake. After picking up furs for trade on Lake Michigan, the Griffon began its return trip. It was never seen again.

Settlement came slowly to the shores of Lake Erie. Not until after the War of 1812 did towns really begin to take root. On the American side, immigrants from Germany, Italy, Finland and central Europe came to work in the quarries and vineyards. On the Canadian side, the Irish and Scots were the first to settle. The great cities — Toledo, Cleveland, Erie, Buffalo — began to emerge, often aided by a strategic location on a good harbor, a railroad line or a canal.

The lake has long been important for shipping, commerce and the well-being of those living on its shores. In a year's time nearly 20 million tons of iron ore alone make their way over the lake, insuring a living for half a million people. Coal from the mines of West Virginia arrives at the shore by rail to make the journey over water to Canadian and American ports. Eleven million people depend on the lake for drinking water. But now, more than ever before, people are finding that Lake Erie has something else to offer — recreation and natural beauty.

Using this book

This is a book about the lesser known parts of the lake. You will not find anything about Toledo, Cleveland, Erie or Buffalo. Information on these cities is abundant and easy to find in other guidebooks and from the Visitors and Convention Bureau in each location.

The book is divided into six chapters, each focusing on a different geographic areas. Each chapter is further divided into sections titled *"Places," "Natural Attractions"* and *"Diversions."*

In *"Places,"* you'll find information about the small towns on the lake shore. Historical background is given, not with the intention of providing a comprehensive history, but to give some perspective on how each town fit into the general pattern of growth along the lake. There is information on attractions — and these are more likely to be museums or lighthouses than miniature golf or go-cart tracks, which may be here today but gone tomorrow. Many of these attractions are closed during the winter or have abbreviated hours, so it is always best to call when planning a visit.

With most towns, there is also a listing of places to eat and places to stay. The restaurants may be elegant, though they are more often not, but common to all is their uniqueness — you won't find a clone in another town. In other words, these are family-owned restaurants, not chains. The same can be said for the accommodations listed. Most are bed and breakfasts, though there are a few inns, cottages and small motels. In all cases they offer something that won't be found in the next place down the road.

The owners are friendly, helpful and eager to please. But they do set their own rules. Some welcome children, some don't. Some accept credit cards, others don't. A few do not permit alcohol on the premises. Many prohibit smoking. Most will not house your pet. Be sure to ask if any of these is a concern. While most places listed remain open all year, a few close for the winter. In nearly all cases, if there doesn't seem to be anything that suits your needs, there is a chain motel within close range. Just call or write the chamber of commerce listed with each town.

There are dozens of nature preserves, state parks, wildlife areas, provincial parks and even one national park on the shore of Lake Erie. Information about these can be found in *"Natural Attractions."* A note of caution: deer ticks that can carry Lyme disease have been found in many areas along the lake. More specific information can be obtained from each park office, but it's a good idea to take precautions if hiking through underbrush. Wear long pants tucked into socks and a long sleeved shirt. Use insect repellent and check yourself after returning from your hike.

"Diversions" lists attractions and interesting places that are not on the lake but are a short drive inland. These may be historical sites, wineries, parks, shopping districts, or sometimes even entire towns.

It doesn't matter if you plan to explore the lake by bike, by car or by foot — or for a day, a week or a month. You'll find plenty to appreciate. *Enjoy.*

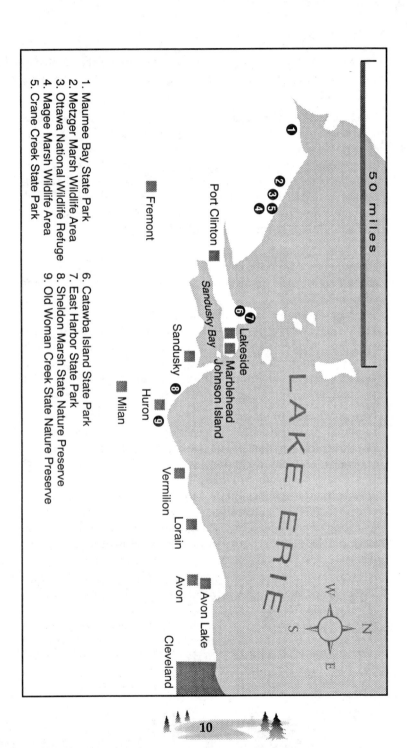

50 miles

LAKE ERIE

1. Maumee Bay State Park
2. Metzger Marsh Wildlife Area
3. Ottawa National Wildlife Refuge
4. Magee Marsh Wildlife Area
5. Crane Creek State Park

6. Catawba Island State Park
7. East Harbor State Park
8. Sheldon Marsh State Nature Preserve
9. Old Woman Creek State Nature Preserve

Fremont

Port Clinton

Sandusky Bay

Sandusky

Huron

Milan

Lakeside
Marblehead
Johnson Island

Vermilion

Lorain

Avon

Avon Lake

Cleveland

Chapter *One*

Western Ohio
The Buckeye State Playground

Thousands of people flock to northwestern Ohio each year, earning it the title of Lake Erie Vacationland. Many head for the nearby islands of Put-in-Bay, Middle Bass or Kelleys Island. But the coastal towns have their appeal too. There's Sandusky, with its famous amusement park, Cedar Point. There's Marblehead, home of one of the oldest and most picturesque lighthouses on the lake. There's Vermilion, with its lovely system of lagoons, great shopping and excellent French restaurant. Natural attractions abound, including state parks, wildlife areas and nature preserves, as well as Ottawa National Wildlife Refuge, the only national refuge in Ohio. For the sun and sand set, there are plenty of beaches.

For kids there's an almost unbelievable array of attractions, most of which adults will probably find unbearably hokey. But what the heck — you can stand a game of miniature golf, a walk through a prehistoric forest inhabited by giant dinosaurs, or a drive through a simulated African savanna complete with animals, can't you? Summer around the western basin is alive with kids and their parents doing just these kinds of things.

The fun doesn't stop when the leaves fall. Autumn and winter bring such events as a Woollybear Festival, Johnny Appleseed Festival, the Great Black-Backed Gull Watch, and a Wood Carving Festival. The holiday season ushers in scenes of lighthouses gently draped with snow, or the beauty of colored lights

TWO-WHEELED JAUNTS

Several areas on Ohio's western shore offer great places for bicycle touring. The Erie County MetroParks has prepared two self-guided tours that begin and end in Huron. The 27-mile Milan Canal Bikeway begins where the Milan shipping canal once entered the lake and parallels the canal's route to its southern terminus at Milan. Along the way are scenic river overlooks, historical sites, the Milan Wildlife Area and rural countryside.

The Lake Shore Electric Trolley Bikeway begins in Huron and travels 11 miles east along the lake to Vermilion, following the route that was once run by the "Lake Shore Electric," the trolley that ran from Cleveland to Toledo beginning in 1899. On its way back to Huron, the bikeway runs south of the lake shore through rural farmland.

Both of these bikeways follow paved roads that are shared with traffic. For maps with annotated points of interest contact Erie MetroParks, 3910 Perkins Ave., Huron, OH 44839; phone 419-625-7783.

One of the most pleasant and scenic places to ride is the approximately eight-mile stretch of Bay Shore Road from the village of Marblehead to Route 269 on the Marblehead Peninsula. The road winds past the Marblehead Lighthouse and the stone house of the first lighthouse keeper, Benajah Wolcott. The causeway to Johnson Island and the Confederate Cemetery runs off from Bay Shore. Farther along, the road passes cottages and little else, but the view of the lake is beautiful. Upon reaching Route 269, you can turn right and go to Route 163, following it east to Marblehead, or you can simply retrace your route.

strung above the Vermilion lagoons, reflected in a broad rainbow over the frozen surface.

When spring comes, so do the birds, headed for summer homes

farther north. One of the best locations in the country for birders, Ohio's western shore supports more than 300 species — vireos, orioles, tanagers, and a host of other avian gems. Waterfowl also are abundant, attracted by the shoreline marshes that dot the coast.

But for a multitude of fishermen, there's one word associated with this part of the lake that brings tremors of anticipation — walleye. The western basin of Lake Erie proudly bears the honor of being the Walleye Capital of the World. The shallowest, warmest and most nutrient-rich section of the lake, this area also produces the most fish. And the most fishermen. They can be seen just after dawn on the coldest of March days, their boats barely visible from shore against the gray of the water. They can be found huddling over holes in the ice every winter. And in the summer, their boats line the horizon like an impenetrable row of sentinels.

There's something for everyone on this part of Lake Erie. And you won't have to search far.

PLACES
Port Clinton

Before white men settled where Port Clinton is today, it was home of the Ottawa, a tribe whose name means "trader," and for whom Ottawa County is named. The Ottawa traded furs and skins for corn and tobacco, living peacefully on the Catawba peninsula, just east of present-day Port Clinton. Then the white men arrived and began to settle. The Ottawa were removed to Kansas by the government in 1831, except for one woman whose daughter, Betsy Mo-John, was to become the last Catawba Ottawa. Her cabin still stands, east of the town.

Port Clinton's name speaks volumes of its ambition as a young town. In 1827, flush with excitement over the Erie Canal between Buffalo and New York, the founders named the town in honor of New York Governor DeWitt Clinton, who had been instrumental in seeing the canal through to its completion.

Port Clinton: Feeding the ducks and gulls near the Jet Express docks.

Whether flattery was a motive or not, they certainly knew that Clinton had proposed a canal from the Portage River, where Port Clinton now stands, to the Ohio River. That the founding fathers named the most westerly thoroughfare Canal Street indicates a certain degree of misplaced confidence. (It was later changed to Harrison Street.)

For, as history played itself out, the powerful won and the canals went to the bigger, more influential towns of Toledo and Cleveland. Port Clinton was forgotten, left to eke out a living from the hardwoods that grew in the forests outside the town. When the wood was gone, the town turned its attention to commercial fishing. When the fish were killed off by pollution, Port Clinton found its present-day niche — tourism.

Port Clinton isn't so much a destination as a jumping-off spot for surrounding attractions. The Jet Express boat whisks fun-seekers to Put-in-Bay daily during the busy summer months. Now that the lake is healthy again, fishermen flock to Port Clinton for the walleye, and bird-lovers come for the spring and fall migra-

Lakeview Park: Dancing on the sandy beach.

tions at nearby Magee Marsh and Ottawa National Wildlife Refuge. Marblehead Peninsula, just to the east, offers quaint shopping and is also the place to catch the ferry to Kelleys Island.

But there are some compliments to be paid to Port Clinton itself. The downtown shopping area, with its wonderful architecture, has retained its vitality, unlike other towns that have lost out to strip centers. Madison Street is lined with gift shops, taverns, restaurants, antique shops, and is the locations of the town's centennial hotel, the Island House. The beach at Lakeview Park is wide and clean. The 1933 Art Deco Whistling Bridge over the Portage River affords a pleasing view of the river traffic and Port Clinton's many marinas. At Waterworks Park next to the Jet Express, you can see a canon used by the British Navy during the famous Battle of Lake Erie in the War of 1812, which was fought nearby.

For lighthouse enthusiasts there's one of the most unusual, and certainly one of the smallest, lighthouses on the lake. Located on the Portage River on the property of Brand's Marina, the tiny wooden Port Clinton Lighthouse guided boats along the river for 90 years after its opening in 1874.

At 126 W. Third Street you'll find the Ottawa County Historical Museum (419-732-2237), managed by the Historical Foundation. All items on display concern Ottawa County life and history and were donated to the museum. They include a collection of Indian artifacts and historical firearms. The museum has extensive historical archives available to researchers. Museum hours are variable so call before dropping by.

Every year on the first weekend of October, Port Clinton celebrates its annual Harvest Festival. There's a food court, live entertainment, craft show, farmer's market and Sunday pancake breakfast. For children, there are clowns, face painting and other events.

Just east of Port Clinton a large peninsula juts eastward into the lake, forming the northern edge of Sandusky Bay. If you look at a map and use your imagination, it looks a bit like a mittened hand, the thumb pointing toward Canada and the rest of the hand pointing due east. These two parts have come to be known by different names — the thumb is Catawba Island (though it isn't an island — just try explaining this to a six-year-old), and the hand is Marblehead Peninsula. Rural Catawba Island is considered part of Port Clinton, though they are as different as night and day.

While Port Clinton is buzzing with revelers heading to the islands and boat traffic in and out of the marinas, Catawba is quiet, much of it farmland given over to peach groves and melon patches. Some of the area's best produce can be found at Catawba's roadside stands in late summer — juicy-sweet peaches, crisp early apples, ripe tomatoes and ears of golden corn.

Catawba has a long history of grape-growing, initiated by European immigrants who discovered that the lake's tempering effect created the ideal climate for the fruit. Mon Ami Winery (419-797-4445 or 1-800-777-4266) was founded in 1872 by these immigrants, who built the winery from local limestone and walnut. While the cellars are still there, complete with giant wooden barrels, no wine is presently produced at Mon Ami. Wines sold under the Mon Ami label are produced at nearby Firelands Winery. Mon Ami today is used as a restaurant and retail outlet, though the cellars can be toured. Next to the winery is the cabin of Betsy Mo-John, last of the Catawba Ottawa.

Part museum, part old-fashioned store, the Ottawa City General Store at 4057 N.W. Catawba Road is an unusual find. Owners Don and JoAnn Rhodes are enthusiastic keepers of local history and will be glad to answer visitors' questions about their collection of artifacts dating from the first settlers to World War I. Side by side with these are cases of penny candy, reels of colorful hair ribbon, and containers of spices, coffees and teas, all of which are for sale. The store is open May through October.

Farther out Catawba Road is the Miller Ferry Dock, where passengers and vehicles embark to Put-in-Bay.

Where to stay:

The Island House
102 Madison Street
Port Clinton, OH 43452
419-734-2166 or
1-800-233-7307

Places like the Island House are few and far between on Lake Erie's shores. Built in 1886, this brick structure is a landmark in downtown Port Clinton. The 39 rooms, all of them different, are decorated with lake motifs. Each room has a private bath, telephone, television and VCR. (Tapes are available for a nominal fee.) In addition to single and double rooms, there are suites that sleep up to eight and include kitchenettes — a great bargain for groups of fishermen or large families. Owners Dave and Pam Waleri have big plans for the Island House. They've already renovated the formal dining room, the more casual grill and many of the guest rooms. The future will bring outdoor dining, a pool, whirlpools and complete spa facilities.

Isle Serene Lodging
216-220 East Perry St.

Port Clinton, OH 43452
419-734-7111

Isle Serene is located on not-so-serene State Route 163 (East Perry Road) smack in the middle of Port Clinton. But for people who want to head for Put-in-Bay, there could hardly be a more convenient location, since it's almost directly across the street from the Jet Express. This is not a B & B — no breakfast is served, and there is no innkeeper or owner on the premises. The eight rooms or suites are located in two remodeled Victorian homes connected by a boardwalk. Each accommodation is different, although all have private bath, TV, air-conditioning and phone. One, the Catawba Suite, has two bedrooms, bath and kitchenette. Rates at Isle Serene drop by almost half after Labor Day — when things are still hopping on the islands. This may be the best time to stay here, when the Catawba Suite rents for under $100 a night. It's a deal, especially in this neighborhood.

Dragonfly Bed and Breakfast and Cottage
1586 Lockwood Road
Port Clinton, OH 43452
419-734-6370

This is the perfect place for kids. In fact, owner Alice, who used to be a teacher, loves having kids around. She's even got a family room stocked with toys. Located on 18 acres south of Port Clinton on the north side of Sandusky Bay, Dragonfly B & B has a quiet, rural setting complete with fishing pond. The pond has lots of crappies, says Alice, and she'll provide the poles. There's also a private beach and an outdoor patio surrounded by Alice's herb garden. Accommodations are four spacious guest rooms and two baths. Cots are available. A cottage that can sleep three (more with cots) and includes a fully equipped kitchen is also on the grounds.

Five Bells Inn
2766 Sand Road
Port Clinton, OH 43452
419-734-1555 or 1-888-734-1555

As if they didn't have enough to do, Pam and Dave Waleri, owners of the Island House, also run this charming B & B on

Catawba Island. "We tried to retire," says Dave. "We failed at it." You could hardly ask for a more perfect location at the lake's edge, where guests can take full advantage of the wide front porch or the chair-swing on the grassy front lawn. Amenities abound at this adult-oriented B & B. The eight rooms all have air conditioning, private baths, TV/VCR and big fluffy robes for guests, and all have been completely sound-proofed. Rates include full home-cooked breakfast, movies and use of bicycles and the outdoor hot tub. There are a paddle boat, rowboat and a canoe for guests to take out on the quiet stretch of the Portage River that borders the property. Dave may even take you for a spin in his vintage Rolls Royce.

SunnySide Tower Bed and Breakfast Inn
3612 N.W. Catawba Road
Port Clinton, OH 43452
419-797-9315

When John Davenport's father sold the home that had been in the family for three generations, John never expected to live there again. But 25 years after the sale, John bought it back again, and with his wife Linda went through the painstaking work of bringing back to life the house which had stood vacant for 30 years. "It was unbelievable," says Linda. "Animals had taken over inside." They spent four years working on the house, attending to it every evening after their "day" jobs. Now they've got a 28-room beauty on rural Catawba Island. The sprawling Victorian farmhouse has six guest rooms, some with private baths, all beautifully decorated. The most unique is the Tower Room, situated as its name implies in a tower above the rest of the house. Guests in the tower have use of the tower porch above their room — a perfect place for stargazing and a midnight toast. John and Linda welcome children, who have plenty of room to play on the spacious grounds. There are 12 acres of woods with trails adjacent to the house. SunnySide Tower is open all year.

Where to eat:

The Island House
102 Madison Street
419-734-2166 or 1-800-233-7307

The Island House has arguably the most elegant dining in town. White tablecloths and chandeliers complement the new blue color scheme, just the right atmosphere for dishes like char-grilled swordfish Provencal, pan-fried rainbow trout or walleye baked with smoked mussels. It's not all seafood, however. There's meat and pasta as well, and a nice wine list to round things out.

Mon Ami Restaurant & Historic Winery
3845 East Wine Cellar Road
1-800-777-4266
419-797-4445

Located on Catawba Island just off Route 53 north of Route 2, Mon Ami is an imposing structure. Built in 1972, the limestone winery began as a co-op run by European immigrants. Today it's owned by Paramount Distillers and the wine is not produced on the premises, but is brought in from nearby Firelands Winery, where it is made. Only the sparkling wine, for which Mon Ami is best known, spends any time at the winery — it is brought

Lakeside: Busy streets and an old-fashioned movie house.

there for aging before it is released for sale. The dining room is casually elegant, serving full entrees as well as salads and sandwiches. In good weather, food and wine are served in a large outdoor courtyard.

Lakeside

There's nothing quite like Lakeside anywhere else on Lake Erie. Founded in 1873 on Marblehead Peninsula by a group of Methodist ministers, it is one of the last surviving "Chautauquas" in the United States. These institutions offer a combination of education, culture, religion and recreation. Lakeside's mission statement says it best: *"To foster traditional Christian values in a Chautauqua setting, to strengthen the quality of family life, and to nurture fellowship by providing programs and services that offer opportunities for enrichment and growth — spiritual, cultural, intellectual and physical — in a restful setting while preserving the timeless quality of Lakeside's heritage."* Today, Lakeside welcomes people of any denomination.

Walking down the street in Lakeside is in many ways like walking into an earlier time. The small Victorian cottages nestle close together, their occupants rocking comfortably on wide front porches. There are few cars, but many families walking, and a few cyclists pedaling down to the lake. The sounds of an orchestra waft from an auditorium and mix with the lapping of waves.

The old-fashioned movie theater has a placard in front advertising one — only one — feature, a movie that would raise no eyebrows even among the grandparent set. There are no bars, no loud music, no jet skis and no flashy tourist attractions. This is Lakeside — the way it's been for years and the way its summer residents wish it to remain.

The season begins in June and ends after Labor Day. During this time, a gate fee is charged ($55 per week per adult, $9 per day per adult; children are less). While this may seem like a lot, the fee entitles visitors to enjoy all the recreational and educational facilities available. These include seminars, workshops, Bible study, swimming, tennis, shuffleboard, ballet and musical performances, other types of entertainment, a supervised playground and a 700-foot fishing dock. Miniature golf, movies and sailboat rental are extra. The Lakeside Symphony is in residence during the summer.

Those who want to learn more about the history of Lakeside and the surrounding area should make a point to stop at the Heritage Hall Museum and Archives on Maple Avenue. The small, well maintained museum, operated by the Lakeside Heritage Society, is housed in the old Lakeside Chapel, built in 1875. There are exhibits on the original Indian inhabitants of the area, local natural history and the development of Lakeside, as well as Lake Erie memorabilia. One of the most interesting offerings of the museum is its Sunday afternoon series of lectures that highlight local history.

Where to stay:

Things are a bit different in Lakeside. The emphasis is on affordable comfort, not luxury, and on family-oriented activities. The result is that places to stay are generally less expensive than you

might expect, but they are also a bit more basic. If you're looking for a romantic getaway, Lakeside is probably not the place. Unlike other areas, children are the rule, not the exception, at B & Bs in Lakeside. Some of the accommodations listed remain open year-round, but most do not.

Rothenbuhler's Guest House
310 Walnut Ave.
Lakeside, OH 43440
419-798-5656

Edith and Marvin Rothenbuhler have been running their guest house for nearly 20 years — and they're still having fun doing it. Their beautiful century home has six guest rooms, three with private baths, all with sinks in the rooms. Some rooms are furnished with pieces original to the house. The Rothenbuhlers serve fresh fruit and home-baked goodies on the large, enclosed, wicker-furnished porch. The atmosphere is family-friendly and cozy. Alcoholic beverages are not permitted.

Idlewyld Bed & Breakfast
350 Walnut Ave.
Lakeside, OH 43440
419-798-4198 (summer)
216-228-8168 (winter)

Probably the most striking thing about Idlewyld is its inviting wrap-around porch with Amish rockers. The century-old house has 15 rooms, five with private baths (though most of these are not self-contained; they consist of a bathroom area enclosed by a privacy screen). All rooms are comfortably furnished and decorated in "country" style. The Rosebud Room even has an old clawfoot tub. Breakfast consists of homemade baked goods, fresh fruit, cereal and beverages. Cooking privileges are available after 10:30 a.m. The back deck has grills and picnic tables for outdoor dining.

Maxwell's Hospitality House
239 Walnut Street
Lakeside, OH 43440
419-798-4527 (summer)
419-864-2921 (winter)

Cecil and Kathryn Maxwell have had many of the same guests return year after year. The Maxwells are gracious hosts, making sure people feel at ease in their home. And their inn is one of best bargains on the lake. Where else can you get a room (at the time of writing) for $18 and up a night? Don't expect anything fancy here — but it's clean, comfortable and cozy — somewhat reminiscent of the guest houses popular around the turn of the century. The rooms have names like the Canary Room, the Rose Room, the Wine Room — all named by Cecil's mother for the original color schemes. (Kathryn is quick to point out that the Wine Room was *not* named for the beverage.) There's a living room with TV and a Steinway baby grand. One room has a half bath; the rest are shared. Coffee is provided in the morning.

The Lakeview Historic Inn and Deli
162 Walnut Ave.
Lakeside, OH 43440
419-798-5845

With the exception of the Hotel Lakeside the Lakeview is the closest accommodation to the lake. Built in the early 1900s, this

restored home has 13 guest rooms, many of which have double and twin beds. Several have attached sitting rooms, and nine include half baths. All are nicely decorated. Air-conditioning is available for a nominal fee. There is a second story deck and enclosed porch. The owners have plans to turn the downstairs deli into a full-service restaurant.

Hotel Lakeside
150 Maple Ave.
Lakeside, OH 43440
419-798-4461

You can hardly miss this Victorian beauty right at the edge of the lake. Built in 1875, the Hotel Lakeside is the third oldest operating hotel in Ohio. Though it's seen hard times, it was restored to its original dignity after a volunteer group, the Friends of Hotel Lakeside, came to its rescue in the 1970s. The 90 rooms are all different, some furnished in priceless antiques. Over the years, the hotel and dining room have seen the likes of Eleanor Roosevelt, Amelia Earhart and Ohio Governor George Voinovich. Though a bit pricier than other Lakeside accommodations, the hotel is still quite reasonable.

For more information contact The Lakeside Association, 236 Walnut Ave., Lakeside, OH 43440; 419-798-4461.

Marblehead

As you drive out Route 163 toward the tip of Marblehead Peninsula, the scene is not very promising. There are trailer parks, gimmicky and unattractive stores, and a few tourist traps only a child could love. But reserve your judgment until you get to the very end and arrive at the village of Marblehead.

You'll find a charming town next to the water, with gift shops, galleries, antique shops and a smattering of small restaurants. Richmond Gallery features the work of local artist Ben Richmond, who is nationally acclaimed for his paintings and drawings of Marblehead and New England seafaring scenery.

During the summer months the Neuman Ferry Dock, located

Marblehead Lighthouse, the oldest in continous operation on the Great Lakes.

The Wolcott House is possibily the oldest building in Northwest Ohio.

right in the town, is bustling with day trippers on their way over to Kelleys Island, just north of Marblehead.

One of the most striking buildings in the village is Holy Assumption Orthodox Church, built in 1898 by early Russian settlers who came to work in the peninsula's limestone quarries. Inside the church are icons given to the congregation by Czar Nicholas II in 1906.

If you continue driving on Route 163, beyond the town and around the tip of the peninsula just beyond the onion domes of St. Mary Byzantine Catholic Church, you will see a small brown sign that says "Marblehead Lighthouse." The narrow drive will take you to one of the most photographed scenes on the Great Lakes. If it's a perfect day, the towering white lighthouse will nearly glow against the backdrop of cerulean sky and aqua water. Built in 1821, it is one of the oldest lighthouses on the

Confederate Soldiers Cemetery, established in 1861.

Great Lakes. When the first lighthouse keeper, Benajah Wolcott, died in 1832, his widow Rachel was appointed to take his place, becoming the first woman keeper in the Great Lakes region. Although the lighthouse is kept locked, tours are given on the second Saturday of each month, spring though fall. The Fresnel lens that was once in the lighthouse is now displayed at the U.S. Coast Guard Station in town. (The public can view the lens without an appointment, but those who would like a tour of the station should call 419-798-4444 to make arrangements.)

Wolcott's house, which historians think may be the oldest existing building in Northwest Ohio, still stands on Route 163 overlooking the water. The Wolcott House, built in the early 1820s, is open to the public several days each summer. Wolcott is buried in the small cemetery behind the house.

Between the lighthouse and the Wolcott House on Route 163 there is a causeway that goes to Johnson Island. Because the island is privately owned, the causeway is also. It costs a dollar to drive over the steep, gravel-covered road, but it's worth it to see the Confederate cemetery just beyond the end of the causeway.

In 1861 the Federal government leased a plot from the island's owner to use as the site for a prison for Confederate officers. There were barracks, a hospital, an arsenal for the guards and a few other buildings surrounded by a 14-foot wall.

Conditions were difficult, especially for men used to a warmer climate. Many died of pneumonia, and the rest nearly died of boredom. The 206 men who died at the camp were buried there, their graves marked only by wooden crosses.

The successful escape of two prisoners one bitter winter night fueled an elaborate plan to take over the prison that contained all the elements of a modern suspense movie — spies, hijackings, smuggled weapons and drugged drinks. The attempt failed, however, and one of the ringleaders was hanged as a result. The other was pardoned.

After the war was over, the camp deteriorated, and today there is nothing left but the cemetery. Now there are white marble headstones instead of crosses, placed there as a gesture of respect by the people of Sandusky in 1890. Many of the graves are marked "Unknown." Yet even today, more than a hundred years after the end of that bitter conflict, it's not unusual to see flowers at the base of a headstone.

The peninsula is home of the only naturally occurring population of Lakeside daisies in the United States. Outside the U.S., Lakeside daisy — the rarest of Ohio's endangered plants — is found only in two remote areas of Canada. The Lakeside Daisy Preserve (1/2 mile south of Route 163 on Alexandria Pike) was established in 1988 for the protection of this colorful flower. In any other season the place looks barren, a lunar landscape of ragged rock. But every spring the yellow blooms of the daisies explode into color at the Lafarge Quarry where the preserve is located. The area is open to visitors only during May; at other times, visitors must apply for a permit from the Ohio Department of Natural Resources Division of Natural Areas and Preserves (614-265-6453).

Where to stay:

The Ivy House
504 Ottawa
Marblehead, OH 43440
419-798-4944 or 798-9361

This charming house was built in the late 1800s by Captain Griesser, an officer at the nearby lifesaving station which is now the U.S. Coast Guard Station. It sits on a wooded lot overlooking the lake in a quiet neighborhood in the village of Marblehead. There are five rooms, all but one with in-room sinks. As the name suggests, the motif throughout is ivy — ivy-covered curtains and slip covers, ivy wallpaper, ivy cups and dishes. Hosts Susan and Ray Lawyer pride themselves on the home-made baked goods and full breakfasts they serve their guests. A special treat awaits guests who take advantage of a day pass the Lawyers provide to a local private club with a mile-long groomed beach.

Old Stone House on the Lake
133 Clemons Street
Marblehead, OH 43440
419-798-5922

You can't get much closer to Lake Erie than the Old Stone House. On a windy day when the lake is stirred up, waves crash over the front patio, drenching the outdoor furniture. But when the lake is behaving, that same spot makes an idyllic place for a peaceful breakfast al fresco. This magnificent home was built by Alexander Clemons in 1861 to house his wife and 14 children. There are 13 guest rooms, including a suite with private bath in a newer wing of the house. The choice room is the Captain's Tower, which was once the "widow's walk" that has since been enclosed. The tower has a private bath and private patio with a spectacular view of the lake. The other rooms, all decorated in different themes, share baths. All guest rooms are air-conditioned. Although the house is open to guests year-round, there is no central heating; each room is equipped with a portable heater. Children over 10 are welcome. The house is within walking distance of the village and ferry docks.

Victorian Inn
5622 E. Harbor Road
Marblehead, OH 43440
419-734-5611

This large mansion, located at the corner of Routes 163 and 269, was built by wealthy fruit farmer Henry Schweck in the late 1800s. The inn can accommodate up to 33 people, and hosts Ann and Wayne Duez often rent the entire house to families for weddings and reunions. There is a large common area that includes a Jacuzzi and outside deck. Ann, who used to own a bakery on Put-in-Bay, enjoys baking for guests and has been known to bake a wedding cake or two. She will also cater meals for an additional fee. The inn offers a number of special events throughout the year, including a New Year's getaway, Valentine's Day special and Murder Mystery weekends.

Where to eat:

Frontwaters Restaurant & Brewing Company
8660 E. Bayshore Rd.
419-798-5914

Located at Lindy's Beach Resort on the south side of the peninsula, Frontwaters is a relaxed place to tip back a few brews and have a nice, but not inexpensive, dinner. The beers, brewed on location, have names like Lightkeepers Ale, Lake Erie's Gale Warning Ale and Marblehead Red. The food is American, with steaks and lake fish figuring prominently.

Mateys Seafood and Chowder House
113 1/2 W. Main St.
419-798-9866

Modeled after New England dockside seafood joints, Mateys offers a good value in a casual setting. It's paper plates and plastic utensils here, where you can eat outside if you wish. Lake Erie perch, walleye, shrimp, oysters and clam chowder are the mainstays.

For more information contact the Peninsula Chamber of Commerce, PO Box 268, Marblehead, OH 43440; 419-798-9777.

Cedar Point and its namesake ferry dock are popular.

Sandusky

Driving into Sandusky, from any direction, gives the impression that all roads lead to Cedar Point. It is this famous amusement park that draws most visitors to the area. But if you bypass the Point and head straight for downtown Sandusky, you'll find there's more to this town than roller coasters and Ferris wheels.

An ill-tempered Charles Dickens passed through Sandusky in 1842 and declared it to be "sluggish and uninteresting." If only he could see it today. With its location on sparkling Sandusky Bay, its lush public gardens and beautiful architecture, it's one of Lake Erie's most impressive towns.

On summer days the harbor is bustling with ferries that carry passengers to Kelleys Island, Put-in-Bay, Pelee Island and across the bay to Cedar Point.

Perched at the edge of one of the largest and most protective bays on the lake, Sandusky has long been an important lake port. But like the rest of the towns on the western side of the lake, things got off to a slow start.

The first white person to set up housekeeping in the area was Michael Gibbs, who built a cabin on the bank of Pipe Creek in 1809. Life was tough in those days, though, and Gibbs only survived for three years before he was killed by Indians.

Things didn't really take off for Sandusky until after the War of 1812 when settlers began drifting in from the East Coast. Sandusky, as well as Huron and Vermilion, is part of the Firelands, a tract of land set aside for New Englanders whose homes had been burned by the British during the Revolutionary War. The town was platted (planned and charted) in 1818 by surveyors who happened to be Masons. They designed the street plan to form the Masonic symbol, and though not all the original streets remain, there are still enough sections of diagonal road to make things confusing.

By 1820 there were 30 houses, four wharves, four warehouses and a ship used for local commerce. Sandusky was not much smaller than Cleveland at the time. In 1828, more than 350 ships docked at Sandusky, many of them to transport Ohio grain. The wide bay made Sandusky an ideal port and location for shipbuilding, and it came to occupy an important position among the towns on the lake.

This growth was not without its glitches. In 1832 cholera arrived in Sandusky. Borne by oceangoing vessels from Europe, the disease spread rapidly along the Great Lakes. 1834 saw another attack, after victims of the disease were dumped from a ship into local waters and subsequently buried by unsuspecting citizens. In 1849 the disease shut the city down, attacking victims both wealthy and poor, causing chaos and panic. The only vestige from these dark days is the cholera victims' cemetery in a residential area on the west side of town.

Like the rest of the American port towns on Lake Erie, Sandusky's growth lagged after Cleveland was chosen as the northern terminus for the canal connecting the lake to the Ohio River. Though the town's role as an important port was thus diminished, two other industries helped spur its development.

Sandusky sits right next door to the most fertile fishing grounds on the lake. The entire western basin, with its shallow, oxygenated water provides a rich environment for spawning. Fishhouses lined Railroad Street by the 1860s, giving the town the nickname, "Fishtown." Fishermen from the entire area brought their catches to Sandusky, where they were transported by rail or ship to cities in the South, East and West. The commercial fishing industry held fast for the first half of the 20th century. Today, though commercial fishing is greatly diminished, Sandusky still attracts thousands of recreational fishermen who come to enjoy the "Walleye Capital of the World."

The other industry that brought prosperity to Sandusky, as well as the surrounding area and the islands, was wine making. German immigrants brought with them their techniques and love of the grape. They found that the rich soil, long growing season and temperate climate was ideal for growing grapes. Although few wineries survived Prohibition, new wineries sprang up after those years, and now the wine industry is alive once again along this part of the lake shore.

Firelands Winery (917 Bardshar Road; 1-800-548-WINE or 419-625-5474), on the west end of town, offers some of the best wine on the lake's western shore. Although the grapes are grown on North Bass Island, the wine is produced at the winery in Sandusky. Firelands is known for its wines made from Vinifera grapes — Chardonnay, Riesling and Cabernet Sauvignon — many of which have won awards over the years. The winery also produces sparkling wines, including a Brut Rose made from Pinot Noir grapes. There is a gift shop and tasting room where helpful staff will make recommendations and answer questions. During the warm months, the garden behind the tasting area is open and snacks are available. There is also a self-guided tour through the winery.

Just down the road a bit, where State Route 2 and U.S. 6 intersect, is a large barn-like building. You can't miss the sign that says Steuk's Country Market and Winery (419-625-0803). Steuk's is one of Ohio's oldest wineries and has been owned and operated by the same family since its founding in 1855. The winery is perhaps best known for its Black Pearl wine, made from the

Artisan at the Merry-Go-Round Museum, Sandusky, Ohio.

grape of the same name. Steuk's is the only producer of this sweet, rich red wine, which is the only wine made from grapes grown on the property (other grape varieties are bought from growers in New York). They also sell fresh-pressed cider and a number of specialty food items. There is a bed and breakfast on the property that overlooks a pond and the Black Pearl vineyard. These are friendly folks who welcome visitors and will be glad to let you taste the wines.

Much of Sandusky's historic architecture has been preserved, especially downtown around Washington Park (a large area reminiscent of the New England "village green"), along the waterfront and on Columbus Avenue, a tony residential street. A brochure that details a downtown walking tour has been prepared by the Old House Guild of Sandusky and is available at the museums in town and at the visitors bureau on Washington Row just across from the park.

Although the onslaught of shopping malls and strip centers caused most downtown merchants to close their doors, specialty shops are beginning to spring up along Market Street, one block from the water. You'll find gift shops with a nautical theme, a children's bookstore, an interior design shop and several other interesting places.

The focal point of downtown, though, is Washington Park. In the summer months it blooms with carefully tended gardens and tropical foliage, which is grown in the city's greenhouse during the winter months. The Boy with the Boot Fountain stands in the middle of the park. It is a bronze replica of a 19th-century statue that is now found in the city building. The original stood in another park, but when the owner died, he willed it to the city. It was damaged in a 1924 tornado but was repaired and placed in Washington Park. After the statue was damaged by vandals in 1991, it was moved to the city building and the replica placed in the park. It has become the symbol of Sandusky. At the northeast corner of the park is the Little Red Wagon, a concession stand that was once horse drawn. It now has a permanent home on the square.

Across from the park on the northwest corner is the former post office which now houses the Merry-Go-Round Museum (419-626-6111). The Neo-Classic style building, unusual for its round shape, seems a perfect place for a museum that focuses on the familiar ride that is also round. The exhibits change, since most are on loan, but the biggest attraction, a restored 1930s Allen Herschell carousel, has a permanent home there. Visitors may ride the carousel. Another permanent fixture is a reconstructed workshop from the Gustav Dentzel Caroussell Builder Shop that operated in Philadelphia beginning in 1867. All of the artifacts and tools are authentic.

Throughout the museum are individual animals in various stages of restoration, some from Europe but most from now-defunct amusement parks around the Midwest and Ontario. Don't think you'll see just horses with wild eyes and flowing manes. At any given time there may be tigers, giraffes, deer, goats, and even a pig. Tucked away in the corner of the museum is a workshop where present-day carvers and artisans sand, carve, paint and cajole animals back to their original state.

The museum has a unique program that works to everyone's benefit. Collectors may bring animals in need of restoration to the museum, where staff carvers will refurbish the animal for free. In return, the owner agrees to loan the restored animal to the museum for a set period of time. Everyone wins. The museum has a constant turnover in new exhibit items, collectors end up with beautiful (and considerably more valuable) results, and a steady stream of historic artifacts are saved from ruin.

Although the museum is open all year, hours vary so call for information. It is closed on Mondays, except during the busy season Memorial Day through Labor Day. Guided tours are available. There is also a small gift shop that sells merry-go-round memorabilia.

Southeast of the park, at the corner of Wayne Street and East Adams, is the Follett House Museum (419-627-9608), operated by the Sandusky Library. Built in the mid-1800s, the Greek Revival mansion is considered one of the finest of its type in Ohio. The museum includes exhibits highlighting the history of Sandusky and Erie Counties and Johnson Island, the site of a prison for Confederate officers during the Civil War.

Artifacts include Indian relics, china, glassware, Victorian furniture and period apparel. There is a Weaving and Spinning Room containing spinning wheels and hand-woven fabrics. The Toy and Doll Room displays 50 dolls, doll houses and other toys. The collection of Johnson Island memorabilia includes letters, photographs and drawings from the Confederate prison just across the bay from Sandusky. Visitors are permitted to climb the stairs up to the "Captain's Walk," where they can view a panorama of the city and lake. The museum also houses a collection of archival materials available to researchers. During the Christmas season, many visitors come to view the decorated trees, garlands, wreaths and other holiday decorations. The museum is open limited hours April through December, closed January, February and March. Call for times.

More than 150 years ago the Eleutheros Cooke House (419-627-0640) stood at the corner of Washington Row and

"The Boy with the Boot Fountain" in Sandusky, Ohio.

Columbus Avenue. Cooke, Sandusky's first lawyer and one of its most prominent citizens, was a founding member of the Firelands Historical Society which was formed in 1857. He and his wife lived in the house until his death; she stayed on until her passing, 14 years later.

The house changed ownership, passing to the Sloane family, prominent members of Sandusky society. When Thomas Sloane, son of the owner, married Sarah Cooke, granddaughter of Eleutheros and Martha Cooke, the house was given to them as a wedding present. But it no longer stood at the corner of Washington and Columbus. It had been dismantled, moved and rebuilt, stone by stone, at its present location, 1415 Columbus Avenue, a residential area south of downtown.

The house changed hands once more before Randolph and Estelle Dorn purchased it in 1951. They set about remodeling it and then lived in it until Randolph's death in 1965. Once again, it was a widow's home until Estelle died in 1994. She willed the house to the Ohio Historical Society, which now owns the property.

The house today, including all its furnishings, looks much as it did the day Estelle died. Volunteers painstakingly took inventory of the items, replacing hairbrushes, hand mirrors and clothing where they had been found. Although the furnishings are a somewhat incongruous mixture of 1950s styles and antiques and fine reproductions, they are generally a testament to the Dorn's good taste. Estelle's beautiful collection of cranberry and ruby glass adorns the living room; the hallway is guarded by a grandfather clock, circa 1800, and reflected in the fanciful Venetian glass mirror.

The house and backyard greenhouse are open to the public; guided tours are available. It is managed by the Old House Guild of Sandusky, a non-profit organization that assists with preservation and restoration of local historic structures. It is open Tuesday through Sunday year-round; closed on Mondays and holidays.

The Sandusky Area Maritime Center (419-624-0274), 279 E. Market Street, occupies a small store-front close to the bay. Lyman boat enthusiasts will appreciate the memorabilia of these classic wooden pleasure boats that were built in Sandusky. Photos of old passenger ferries that once operated from Sandusky to Cedar Point or the islands line the walls. There are artifacts, including an old diving suit once used by Neuman Boat Line, as well as old ice cutting tools used in the days before refrigerators, when ice cut from frozen Sandusky Bay was big business. Some models of lake freighters and passenger ferries are also on display. Hours vary, and the museum is closed January through March.

Cedar Point Amusement Park (419-627-2350) is by far the biggest draw to Sandusky. During the season (mid-May through Labor Day; weekends in September), local hotels and restaurants are jammed, and lodging reservations must be made well ahead of time. The park's parking lot is overflowing and lines for the rides are long. But what sets Cedar Point apart from the plethora of American amusement parks is its beautiful location on a narrow strip of land that juts out into Lake Erie.

This narrow spit of sand has been attracting picnickers, sun-bathers and swimmers ever since the area has been inhabited. (You can still do these things, but you must pay a park admission.) Cedar Point's predecessor opened here in 1870. Ferries carried revelers from Sandusky across the bay, making a trip to the Point that much more attractive. Beginning in the late 1800s, excursion boats ran regularly between Cleveland and Cedar Point.

But by 1956 the park's future didn't look bright. It had fallen into disrepair, was sold and then slated for destruction to make way for a residential development. Just about the same time, Disneyland was enjoying enormous success. Cedar Point's new owners took a long look at this phenomenon and decided it was worth making another go of it.

They sank millions of dollars into renovation and landscaping. It worked. Saved from the wrecking ball, the park became one of the area's biggest sources of revenue — and supplied many a child with first memories of a great blue lake viewed from the top of a giant Ferris wheel.

Today you'll find the same litany of rides as at most large amusement parks, such as the roller coasters that turn you inside out (there are 12 of them), but Cedar Point will always remain distinctive for its choice home.

Where to stay:

There are accommodations galore in Sandusky, and they range from the somewhat seedy-looking to major national hotel chains. You can easily spend $100 a night on a "you've seen one, you've seen 'em all hotel room." But why do that, when you can spend less money and stay in one of the town's truly unique B & Bs? They are pricier than some in other areas, but generally they are less than a hotel room. And don't forget that breakfast is included. So unless you've got a kid or two (who would be much happier with a pool and game room anyway), give one of these a whirl. Things book up quickly in Sandusky, especially in the summer, so be sure to make reservations. Most of the B & Bs take credit cards, but not all, so be sure to ask. Most require deposits.

The Cottage Rose
210 W. Adams Street
Sandusky, OH 44870
419-625-1285

The Cottage Rose really looks like a cottage — one of those charming English affairs from a D.H. Lawrence novel. And there are roses, lots of them, prompting owners Susan and Virgil Hahn to coin the motto, "and the smell of the roses still linger." It's a bit like walking into a museum when you enter The Cottage Rose. It is furnished with heavy Victorian pieces, and decorated with hats and feathers and other Victoriana ("I love it," says Susan, "and this gives me such an excuse to have it.") Some of the house's original silk damask wall coverings and draperies remain, and the Hahns have taken a special interest in installing antique light fixtures. Guests have the use of the second floor, where there are two bedrooms, a sitting room and a shared bath. The Hahns prefer to rent to just one couple at a time, or to two couples who know one another. Victorian parlor readings are available by appointment.

The Red Gables
421 Wayne Street
Sandusky, OH 44870
419-625-1189

When Jo Ellen Cuthbertson was a child, she loved to visit her father's medical practice, housed in a great old mansion. She admired the high ceilings, the oak woodwork, the fireplaces, and the spacious upstairs rooms that were used as a dormitory for nurses. Now Jo Ellen lives in the house that she converted to a B & B. The Great Room, where her father's practice used to be, is used as the common area, dining room, and party room on occasion. Upstairs there are four rooms, two with private baths, the other two with a shared bath. Despite the large room sizes, the feeling here is one of coziness, due largely to the chintz slip-covers, comforters and curtains handmade by Jo Ellen. Many of the original bathroom fixtures have been preserved, including a couple of beautiful marble sinks and a toilet with embossed designs. Ohio Governor Voinovich and his wife once stayed here. "They were lovely," says Jo Ellen.

Simpson-Flint House
234 E. Washington St.
Sandusky, OH 44870
419-621-8679

Located just two blocks from the bay, the Simpson-Flint House is an example of 1890 Queen Anne style. Owners Cynthia and Jon Komarek are known for their full breakfasts featuring eggs benedict and home-made muffins. Perhaps the most stunning feature of the downstairs are the stained glass windows that line the living and sitting rooms. There are fireplaces scattered throughout the house, which is furnished with antiques. In fact, antiques are a special hobby of the Komareks' — they have refinished much of the furniture themselves. There are three guest rooms, each with private bath and air conditioning. If you have a choice, ask for the Green Room. It is spacious and bright, with a cozy sitting area by a bay window and a bathroom you could run laps in. There is also a small apartment with a separate entrance available. It can sleep four (in two double beds). Breakfast is not included with rental of the apartment.

The Tea Rose
218 E. Washington St.
Sandusky, OH 44870
419-627-2773

The Tea Rose was built in 1890 as the rectory for nearby Grace Church. The church couldn't afford to maintain the large building, though, and it was sold. By the time Ellen and Andy Kraus bought the house in 1987, the towering Victorian mansion had been divided into seven tumble-down apartments. "Slum real estate at its worst," is how Ellen describes it. You would never believe it today. The couple gutted the place and started from scratch, restoring the home to its original grandeur. There are two large guest rooms, one with a queen-sized bed and sofa bed, the other with a double bed. They share a bath. Both rooms are air conditioned and have cable TV. Downstairs is The Tea Rose Tearoom, where Ellen serves an elegant tea each weekday afternoon (cost not included in B & B rates) and reads guests' tea leaves. She's also been known to do palm readings and tarot card readings for her guests (these also are extra).

1890 Queen Anne Bed & Breakfast
714 Wayne Street
Sandusky, OH 44870
419-626-0391

All of Sandusky's B & Bs have something unique to offer. The 1890 Queen Anne Bed & Breakfast has elegance. Although its size and garroted tower make it impressive from the outside, it's when you take a step into the front door that you'll really let out a sigh of admiration. High ceilings, bright and airy rooms, impeccable decoration and antique furnishings all distinguish the interior of this limestone mansion. Built in the 1890s in the Queen Anne style, it retains a certain quiet grandeur of its age. It is owned by Robert Kromer, whose late wife Joan decorated it. Only one family lived in the house previously — that of John T. Mack, publisher of the town's first newspaper. There are three guest rooms, each with private bath and air-conditioning. In the summer, breakfast is served outdoors on the screened-in porch overlooking a garden.

Wagner's 1844 Inn
230 E. Washington St.
Sandusky, OH 44870
419-626-1726

Several years ago while traveling in Germany, Barb Wagner watched an old woman raking a field of hay. "I need a simpler life," thought Barb, who was then a nurse. Wagner's 1844 Inn was born. This is the oldest building of the B & Bs in town. Built, as its name implies, in 1844, the antique-filled house was once the home of William Simpson, one of Sandusky's early settlers. There are three spacious guest rooms, all with modern, private baths and air conditioning. The second-floor billiard room is equipped with a television and small refrigerator. The place is quiet and conveniently located. Owners Barb and Walt Wagner are gracious hosts, and you may find a surprise by your bedside. Have a weakness for homemade chocolate-covered cherries? This may be your place.

Where to eat:

Margaritaville
212 Fremont Ave.
419-627-8903

What's so unique about this place isn't the food — which is good — it's the location. Built at the site of an 1800s grist mill, it doesn't look like much from the outside. In fact, it looks like there's nothing there at all. You enter a door and walk immediately downstairs below the parking lot level. There you find a lovely scene completely invisible from above — you are at eye level with the rushing water that once powered the mill. Ducks and other waterfowl swim languidly in the peaceful pool beyond.

FOR THE RESORT-MINDED

Those who prefer the amenities of a full-service resort to the intimacy of B & Bs and inns will find what they're looking for on Ohio's northwestern shore. The first three listed here are operated by Cedar Point Resorts (PO Box 5006, Sandusky, OH 44871-5006) and are adjacent to the park. They are open seasonally. Sawmill Creek, which is open year-round, is west of Huron, just a few minutes away.

The Hotel Breakers (419-627-2106), originally built in 1905, is located on Cedar Point Beach. In addition to the lake, there are two heated outdoor pools. Restaurants, gift shops and a game room are on the property. Both rooms and suites are available.

The Sandcastle Suites Hotel (419-627-2107) has its own beach, outdoor pool, whirlpool spa, tennis courts and restaurant. Each suite, which can accommodate up to four people, has a screened-in patio or balcony and refrigerator.

The Radisson Harbour Inn (419-627-2500) is located on the waterfront at the entrance to Cedar Point. All rooms or suites have screened-in balconies or patios. The hotel features an indoor pool, whirlpool, exercise and game rooms, restaurant and a children's center. There is no beach.

You could check into Sawmill Creek Resort (2401 Cleveland Road West, Huron, OH 44839; 419-433-3800) spend a week, and never leave the property. There are 240 rooms and suites, meeting rooms, restaurants, lounge, marina, tennis courts, swimming pools, shops and an 18-hole golf course. Its isolated location right on the lake makes this an appealing place.

The fare is Mexican-American, the portions are huge, the prices are reasonable. And you can't beat the view.

For more information contact the Sandusky/Erie County Visitors and Convention Bureau, 231 W. Washington Row, Sandusky, OH 44870; phone 1-800-255-ERIE or 419-625-2984.

Huron

When John Baptiste Flemmon set up housekeeping in his two-room cabin on the Huron River in 1805, Huron became the first town settled in the Firelands. Like the rest of the Firelands, not much happened in Huron until after the War of 1812, and even then things were slow going.

Like its rivals Sandusky and Vermilion, Huron set out to be a ship-building town and lake port. It was second choice, however, among many captains who preferred to harbor in the wide protected waters of Sandusky Bay than to risk the shallow-water approach to Huron. Passengers destined for Huron often found themselves docked at Sandusky and had to find their way overland back east to get there.

One of the most famous ships built at Huron was the steamer Great Western, which was launched in 1838. It had both paddle

Captain Montague's Bed and Breakfast, Huron, Ohio.

wheels and sails, and was the first steamer on the lake with cabins above the main deck. Well-heeled passengers enjoyed the upper cabins and promenades surrounding them, while the below-deck quarters housed immigrants headed west in search of new lives.

Things looked a little grim for Huron when the industrious little town of Milan, to the south, built a canal to the lake and proceeded to capture most of the shipping business. Then, when the railroads bypassed Milan and the village began to lose its grip on trade, Huron revived. In addition to the ship-building industry, Huron became an important port for the transport of coal, iron ore, lumber and other goods. Fishing and ice harvesting also contributed to the town's economy.

Today, for most of the year, Huron is a quiet place. The port still hosts cargoes of ore, stone and grain, but the shipyards are long gone — now the two biggest industries are a paint manufacturer and a producer of automotive plastics. The place turns lively in the summertime, when visitors are drawn by its close proximity to Cedar Point, and boaters are attracted to the many marinas.

The center for summer fun is the Huron Boat Basin and Amphitheater, located just above the mouth of the Huron River. Throughout June, July and August there are concerts festivals, fireworks, flea markets and antique shows at the amphitheater. Several times a month there are free, family-oriented outdoor movies. Short-term, overnight or seasonal dockage is available at the municipal docks, or at several private marinas farther upriver.

Just west of the river is Huron's "mile-long pier," which is actually only a half-mile long. (The idea is that if you walk to the end, then back again, you've walked a mile on the pier.) The pier is bordered on the west by what looks like a large pile of dirt that's been dropped out of the sky — which actually isn't too far from the truth. Seventy acres' worth of dredging material from the Sandusky and Huron harbors has been placed here. When completely filled, the area will be turned into a park.

There are two public beaches in Huron — the small Lake Front Park and Beach at the foot of Ohio Street, and the larger Nickelplate Park and Beach on the east side of the Huron River. Both parks have grills and picnic tables.

James H. McBride Arboretum, located at Firelands College south of Route 6, has 20 acres of decorative plants and plant groupings native to Ohio. The other 30 acres of grounds include meadows, woods and a lake. In the spring the arboretum draws visitors who come to see the 150 crab apple trees in bloom.

While not known for shopping like its neighbor, Vermilion, Huron has a couple of very interesting places for you to part with your money. Wileswood Country Store (Cleveland Road East and Huron Street; 419-433-4244) offers, as the cliche goes, a step into the past. More than 25 years ago Addison and Ozelma Frey Wiles decided to open the store, based on childhood memories of Huron's General Store where they had shopped with their parents when they were children. The store is run today by Sue and Charles Cloak, who claim to be purveyors of over 5,000

Inland Seas Maritime Museum in Vermilion, Ohio.

unusual items that might have been found in a general store during the late 1800s and early 1900s. There's plenty for kids — candy, dolls and toys — with nary a battery in sight.

On the more sophisticated (and pricey) side, you'll find the 1887 Shops at Sawmill Creek Resort (2401 Cleveland Road West; 419-433-5402), just east of town. The shops, which are actually different sections under one roof, are housed in a barn built in 1887 on the grounds of a farm that had been established in the early 1800s. In 1969 the property was purchased by a business group from Cleveland who built the resort complex known today as Sawmill Creek Resort. They left the barn intact and incorporated it into the resort as a shopping area. The original walnut and oak beams remain, held together not by nails but by wooden pegs. The feeding troughs for the farm animals can still be seen, surrounded by gourmet food items and designer clothes.

For those who want to learn more about Huron's past, the Huron Historical & Cultural Center (419-433-4660), located at 401 Williams Street, is open April through Labor Day, on week-

One of Vermilion's many gift shops.

ends and Wednesdays. Displays and exhibits change periodically.

Where to stay:

Captain Montague's
229 Center Street
Huron, OH 44839
419-433-4756
1-800-276-4756

A few years ago Judy and Mike Tann were looking for a condo, something small and tidy since their two sons were grown. Captain Montague's was on the market at the time, put up for sale by the couple who had brought the house back from the brink of decay and made a showcase of it. But only the people who stayed there ever saw the inside of it. Judy was more than a bit curious. She asked her agent to take her through "just for a look" and the rest, as they say, is history. Judy and Mike's lovely B & B still has a few of its original features from the 1870s, like the carved black walnut staircase and fireplace mantles built into the house by its first owner, who also owned the local lumberyard. The house is filled with antiques and decorated in exquisite Victorian style. There are seven guest rooms, including a spacious bridal suite, each with private bath and air conditioning. A gazebo and in-ground swimming pool surrounded by a garden add to the relaxing ambiance.

For more information contact the Huron Chamber of Commerce, 417 Main Street, Huron City Building, Huron, OH 44839; phone 419-433-5700.

Vermilion

Vermilion, situated at the mouth of the Vermilion River, is one of the prettiest towns on the lake. With its black and white salt-box houses built on a system of lagoons, this town named for the red clay found on the river banks resembles a New England village. The restored area along Liberty Street is lined with small shops and eateries. You can find just about everything in Vermilion, from homemade chocolates to high-fashion clothes, from antiques to fine art, from handicrafts to Old World music boxes and porcelain dolls.

Although the town has lived quietly in the shadow of Cleveland for more than a hundred years, it wasn't always that way. In the mid-1800s, Vermilion had thriving shipyards and was home for more than 50 lake captains. One of its most famous mariners was Captain Alva Bradley.

Bradley came to Vermilion in the 1820s with his Connecticut parents when he was nine years old. The son of a farmer, he worked the fields, but always with an eye on the lake. When he was 19, he landed a job as cook's helper on a lake schooner, and a lifelong love for the lake was born. He was a natural sailor and a shrewd businessman. He eventually came to own the ship he'd signed onto.

Among Bradley's friends were Samuel and Nancy Edison, who had left Ontario to settle in Milan, Ohio, where Samuel operated a mill. When their son was born in 1847, they named him

Thomas Alva in honor of Captain Bradley. It was Bradley who got Thomas a job at Port Huron, where the future inventor first became intrigued by electricity.

Meanwhile, Bradley launched into the shipbuilding business. He built his first ship, the South America, at Vermilion in 1841. Every year more ships were added to his fleet until he became one of the most prominent builders on the lake, bringing notoriety to the pretty port at the mouth of the river. But the lure of Cleveland, with its promise of wealth and prestige, was more than Bradley could resist. He moved his offices to the larger city in 1859, and his shipyards in 1898. It marked the beginning of the end for Vermilion's glory days as a shipbuilding town. Bradley's Vermilion home, built in 1840, still stands at 5679 Huron Street.

Long after Sandusky, Port Clinton and the islands had become tourist attractions, Vermilion was content to sit on the sidelines, quietly minding its business. By the mid-1900s its downtown buildings were decaying, its streets unkempt. Concerned citizens, though, were not about to let the blight continue unabated. In 1967, Theodore Wakefield and the Friends of Harbour Town Committee commissioned a restoration plan from the Lorain Regional Planning Commission. With the support of the mayor, these citizens formed The Friends of Harbour Town, a private, non-profit restoration organization, and the revitalization of the town was underway.

Over the years, The Friends of Harbour Town have raised thousands of dollars, through fund-raisers and appeals, which have gone toward the restoration project. All efforts have been volunteer, the work of "the common man," as Executive Director Diane Chesnut points out. The results are visible in today's restored historical district, Harbour Town 1837, so-named for the year in which the town was incorporated.

Liberty Street, the main road that parallels the lake, is where much of the work has been done. One of the first buildings to be restored was what is now The Harbour Store. Built in 1847, it is believed to be the oldest surviving structure in the downtown area. Over the years it has served as a doctor's office, drug store, grocery store, bicycle shop, dentist's office, pool hall and the mayor's office. The owner, Margaret Worcester, also restored her home, Captain Bradley's old house on Huron Street.

Also on Liberty Street is The Captain's Chair, which has been a barbershop since 1868. Though probably not a part of 19th century decor, it sports an old-fashioned red, white and blue striped barber pole. Across the street is William's Law Office, in a restored 1907 building. Higgin's Pharmacy, down the street from The Captain's Chair, used to be the old Hart's Drug Store. Though its wares are modern, it still has an old soda fountain. Built in 1870, it was originally a dry goods store.

Farther west on Liberty Street you'll find Old Jib's Corner, an 1860 house named for Jib Snyder, a local sailor and fisherman. It houses the offices of The Friends of Harbour Town as well as a gift shop and restaurant.

Restored captain's homes, with their Victorian gingerbread, are scattered throughout the residential streets. A map with self-guided walking tour is available from The Friends of Harbour Town.

The Friends of Harbour Town also offers one-day guided bus tours of historic Vermilion for senior citizens, school groups or any other interested parties.

Several annual weekend festivals draw visitors to the town. Summer kicks off with the Festival of the Fish each June. Lake Erie perch sandwiches are the fare of the day, enjoyed in a carnival-like atmosphere. In August, Antiques and Artists in the Park takes place in the Farmer's Exchange Park on Liberty Street. Nautical exhibits and displays, historic vehicles, antiques and arts and crafts are featured.

The biggest to-do may be the annual Woollybear Festival held each year in October. Ostensibly in honor of the woollybear caterpillars whose numbers supposedly predict the severity of the coming winter, it's all just an excuse to have a big party. There's live music, Woollybear King and Queen costume contests, caterpillar races, local television personalities and a huge parade featuring some 30 marching bands.

Whether they come for one of these special weekends or just a visit, many people arrive in Vermilion by boat. In addition to private yacht clubs, the city has public guest docks on the Vermilion River that can accommodate 20 power or sailboats up to 50 feet long. Water and electricity are available, and there are rest rooms and showers.

Those without their own boat can sail the lake on board the windjammer, Friendship. The ship, typical of the sloops used by Vermilion fishermen in the last century, can accommodate twelve people. During the season, it sails in the afternoon and again in the evening for a sunset sail. For information and reservations call 440-967-WIND.

Cruises also depart every evening from McGarvey's Dockside Restaurant aboard the Mystic Belle. These half-hour excursions take passengers on a narrated cruise through the harbor and lagoons. Call Blue Finn Charters at 440-322-6902 for information.

Perhaps the biggest steady draw to Vermilion is the impressive Inland Seas Maritime Museum (440-967-3467), established in 1953 by the Great Lakes Historical Society. Originally confined to the former Wakefield Mansion, the museum has since added a wing and undergone restoration. In addition to its many displays and artifacts, the museum also houses the Clarence S. Metcalf Library, the largest collection of books, periodicals, drawings and records pertaining to Great Lakes history. Although books and materials cannot be loaned, they are available for on-site research.

In the museum wing there are timbers from Perry's flagship, the Niagara, paintings, models, navigational instruments, a life-sized replica of a captain's bunk and the Fresnel lens from the Spectacle Reef Lighthouse on Lake Huron. The lens, which was dismantled in 1982 by the Great Lakes Historical Society and reassembled in Vermilion, is a second-order Fresnel, invented by French physicist Augustin Fresnel in the early 1800s. According to the display, "the development of the Fresnel lens significantly reduced the number of lamps required for each lighthouse, while magnifying and concentrating the remaining light exponentially." The lenses are classed by size, first-order being the most powerful and standing six to ten feet tall.

At the rear of the museum is the original pilothouse from the steamer Canopus, built in 1905. It was used to carry cars from Detroit to Cleveland from 1950 to 1961 before it was acquired by the museum in 1992.

A full-sized replica of the 1877 Vermilion lighthouse stands on the museum grounds overlooking the lake. The original lighthouse was built on the bank of the Vermilion River in 1877, but was dismantled in 1929 and moved to eastern Lake Ontario, where it now stands.

The museum is open daily, year-round, except on holidays.

Where to stay:

Capt. Gilchrist Guesthouse
5662 Huron Street
Vermilion, OH 44089
440-967-1237

Not long ago, the Victorian mansion that is now the Capt. Gilchrist Guesthouse was an apartment building. Among its tenants were Dan and Laura Roth. It was their dream to buy the former home of shipping magnate J. C. Gilchrist and restore it to its original 1885 charm. They did so, with loving care, and today it's one of the prettiest B & Bs on the lake. In 1992 it was featured in the coffee-table book, America's Painted Ladies. The Roths live downstairs, but the second floor has been converted to three guest rooms surrounding a large common area. Each room has a private bath, and one room has its own kitchen for those staying longer than overnight. It is furnished with antiques and decorated with nautical artifacts. The guesthouse is adjacent to the Inland Seas Maritime Museum and a short walk to downtown businesses.

Where to eat:

Chez Francois

555 Main Street
440-967-0630

This is one of the finest restaurants anywhere on Lake Erie, of a quality almost unheard of in such a small town. The mid-1800s building on the shore of the Vermilion River was once a sail loft. There's not a nail to be found in the ceiling beams, which are held together with wooden pegs. The cuisine is French, as the name implies, and while it's not inexpensive, it's quite a good value. Customers are asked to dress appropriately (which means a jacket if you're a man; no ties required) for the main restaurant, though in the summer months there's an outdoor cafe that is more casual. The restaurant closes each year on January 1 and remains closed until mid-March.

Old Prague Restaurant
5586 Liberty Ave.
440-967-7182

Eating here is almost like dining in someone's home. In fact, it almost is home for the owner, Vera, whose family has been involved with the restaurant since the early 1970s. If you're a stranger to Czech food, just ask Vera or one of the staff — they'll be happy to give you a detailed description of ingredients and preparation, and make recommendations that fit your tastes. This is the food you love, but know you probably shouldn't eat (at least not on a daily basis). There's roast pork with sauerkraut, chicken swimming in creamy paprikash sauce, wiener schnitzel with mashed potatoes, and for dessert — simply put, the best homemade apple strudel you may ever taste. Hours vary with the seasons, so call first.

For more information contact the Vermilion Chamber of Commerce at 5495 Liberty Ave., Vermilion, OH 44089; 440-967-4477. Contact the Friends of Harbour Town at 5741 Liberty Ave., Vermilion, OH 44089; 440-967-4262.

Lorain

Just 30 miles west of Cleveland, Lorain lies in the shadow of that larger city's prominence. Yet Lorain has a distinguished history

"The Jewel of the Port," Lorain, Ohio.

as one of the lake's great industrial centers. It may also be the quintessential hard luck town.

Located at the mouth of the Black River, Lorain (known in turn as Black River, Charleston, Black River again and finally Lorain — for the Lorraine province in France) was settled in the early 1800s and quickly became known for its excellent harbor. A ship-building industry sprang up, along with a lively commerce shipping locally grown grain to other ports on the lake.

When the location of the northern terminus of the Ohio and Erie Canal was being debated, Lorain held its breath along with the other major lake towns, though its citizens were sure that the town's prime harbor would be the determining factor. But it was to be otherwise, and Lorain languished.

Later, the town pricked up its ears at the prospect of an East-West railway running through Lorain, but the honor went farther south to Elyria. With this setback, the settlement nearly disappeared as people moved away to be closer to the centers of commerce.

There were other problems. By 1890, the town still had no paved roads and was plagued by malaria and typhoid fever, giving it the reputation of a disease-ridden mud hole. When the Town Council determined that sewers would solve the health problems of Lorain's citizens, sewers were commissioned and built. The death rate tripled. It didn't take long for someone to figure out that the sewers had been placed only two-thirds of a mile from the water supply intake.

The 20th century ushered in a new age for Lorain — one of industry. All across the American side of the lake, steel mills were starting up, and with its port on the Black River, Lorain was a choice spot. The Johnson Steel Company, now known as USS/Kobe Steel, began operations, attracting workers from neighboring towns and foreign countries. And work they did. The Johnson Company Pay Book for the week ending June 6, 1896, shows that worker number 1141, A. Kernesy, worked 97-and-a-half hours that week. His pay? $14.62. He wasn't the exception — a 40-hour work week was virtually unheard of.

Other industry came to Lorain. The American Ship Building Company, later to become the largest shipbuilding operation on the Great Lakes, opened up shop and turned out ships for the ore fleets, and later, warships and minesweepers for World War II.

Although a 1924 tornado had extracted a heavy toll on the town, Lorain was on a roll. Or so it seemed. Then the town was dealt a severe blow by the closing of the ship company. Other industries followed suit, leaving the town one-by-one. A new Ford assembly plant took up some of the slack, but not enough to keep the town from plunging into hard economic times. Although the steel plant and the auto industry remain, automation has drastically reduced the number of workers, and the threat of moves to other locations where labor is cheaper always hangs in the air.

Since the future for industry looks less than promising, Lorain is turning toward developing its port and lakefront to attract visitors. The city's ambitious plan calls for new public marina facil-

Fishing and family outing at Maumee Bay State Park.

ities, a new lakefront park with sand beach, a hotel and shops. This new awareness of the lakefront's importance has brought a renewed interest in Lorain's lighthouse, "The Jewel of the Port." Built in 1917, the lighthouse is one of the most unusual on Lake Erie. It is large enough to be a house — and indeed it was for the Coast Guard personnel who were posted there. Its white exterior and red roof make a striking sight against the backdrop of the lake. Because it is no longer in use, the lighthouse had fallen into disrepair until the Port of Lorain Foundation bought it and began renovation. Work has begun on the base (constructed, incredibly, of wood); restoration will continue with the exterior and eventually the interior.

The best way to learn about the history of Lorain is to pay a visit to the Black River Historical Society at their museum headquarters. The Moore House, 309 Fifth Street (440-245-2563), was saved from the wrecking ball, restored, and opened to the public in 1995. The house, which was built in 1906, was the residence of Leonard Moore, one of Lorain's mayors. It is remarkable for its American chestnut and pine floors, and for its oak woodwork and staircase. It is filled with displays and artifacts, some unique to Lorain's history, some common to any 19th century Ohio town. There are dozens of "gadgets" — hand washing machines, milk bottles designed to separate cream from the milk, prototype toasters — no doubt considered state-of-the-art in their time. For a couple of dollars you can get guided tour with one of the museum's volunteers, a first-hand capsule history of one of the lake's greatest towns.

Leonard Moore, first owner of the museum that bears his name and one-time Lorain mayor, is responsible for one of the town's most attractive assets. Lakeview Park, to the west of downtown, was once empty countryside outside the city limits. Moore, not yet mayor but active in local politics, thought this land should be acquired and made into a park. The citizens thought he was crazy — why should they be interested in land that wasn't even in Lorain? He fussed and made noise for years, but it took getting elected mayor for anyone to listen to him. Today the beach, edged by the lake on one side and a boardwalk on the other, is the nicest in this part of Ohio.

Where to eat:

Castle Feast Restaurant
2532 W. Erie Ave. (Rt. 6)
440-244-1486

One of the stranger sights along the lake is the large limestone castle that sits on the north side of Route 6 just west of downtown Lorain. Originally a private home, it was built in the 1920s as a replica of a Scottish country house, right down to the thickness of the walls and the floor plans. The tunnel that leads from the cellars down to the lake was also a part of the original plan, one that came in quite handy during the rum-running days of Prohibition. In the 1940s the house became a restaurant, and it has remained one ever since. The ambiance is Medieval but the food is old-fashioned American. Unfortunately the addition of a party room has obscured the view of the lake from the dining room. Nevertheless, it's an interesting place, especially for kids.

For information call Lorain Co. Visitors Bureau, 611 Broadway

Ave., Lorain, OH 44052; 1-800-334-1673 or 440-245-5282.

NATURAL ATTRACTIONS

Maumee Bay State Park

The first two words that come to mind when visiting Maumee Bay just east of Toledo may be "flat" and "barren." There's not much in the way of hills — unless you count the undulations on the golf course — and even less in the way of big, shady trees. But don't turn the page. There's plenty here to appreciate, not the least of which is the newest lodge in the Ohio State Park system.

Quilter Lodge, named for State Representative Barney Quilter, has 120 balconied rooms, most of them overlooking the bay. There are also loft rooms with refrigerators. Close by or in the building are indoor and outdoor pools, racquetball and tennis courts, exercise rooms, saunas, whirlpools, a game room and a dining room with lounge.

The cabins may be even more impressive. These are unique among any in the state parks, and seem more like beach houses than cabins. Each has a gas fireplace, central heat and air, TV, telephone and microwave. There are two-bedroom and four-bedroom units, as well as some cottages that are connected to one another by an elevated walkway, a popular option for large groups. The units are equally appealing in all seasons — open to lake breezes in the summer and cozy in the winter, meaning they are in demand year-round. Get your reservation in early. During the summer months, they are available by the week only.

For those who prefer a more basic stay, there's a 256-site campground. All sites have electricity. There are ample shower and toilet facilities and a laundromat. Three Rent-A-Camp units are available. These are for families who would like to try camping but don't have all the bells and whistles. Each unit is equipped with a tent, propane stove, two cots, camp light and cooler.

There are two swimming beaches in the park, one on Inland

Accessible fishing pier at Metzger Marsh Wildlife Area.

Lake and the other on the bay. Fifty-seven-acre Inland Lake is man-made, stocked with fish and suitable for canoes, sailboats or electric motor boats. The park rents several types of boats, as well as jet skis, which can only be used in the bay.

Golfing enthusiasts will appreciate the 18-hole "Scottish Links" style course and pro shop. In the winter, visitors can cross-country ski, ice skate or go sledding on man-made Big Hill. The park also boasts a marina, an amphitheater for summer entertainment, a nature center and hiking trails.

Three-mile Mouse Trail leads through meadows, marshland and young woodlands, though parts of the trail are paved and shared with bicyclists. A two-mile boardwalk trail begins at Trautman Nature Center, winding through marsh and swamp to an observation tower. A trail guide available at the nature center interprets numbered sites along the boardwalk.

The nature center, staffed by naturalists, offers interactive displays, an auditorium, gift shop and viewing windows. A remote

Ottawa National Wildlife Refuge.

video system in the marsh transmits wetland activities back to the center, allowing a candid glimpse of this rich environment.

For more information contact the park office at 419-836-7758, the camp office at 419-836-8828, or the lodge at 419-836-1466 or 1-800-282-7275.

Metzger Marsh Wildlife Area

The Great Black Swamp, which once blanketed the vast area bordered by Detroit, Fort Wayne and Sandusky, created an almost impenetrable barrier. In spring, the water stood knee-high; in summer the area swarmed with malarial mosquitoes and was full of noxious fumes from rotting vegetation. In all seasons it was a mud-trap for any wagon that tried to traverse it. Although a road was built across it in 1827, few people dared to travel it, so legendary was the swamp's reputation for illness and death. The Black Swamp met its own end, or nearly so, in the later 1800s, when it was ditched and drained to create farmland.

Now cornfields grow alongside Route 2. But not all of the reclamation was successful. In many places the lake refused to give up the marshes on its banks, flooding the areas during high water levels. Efforts to farm this land were relinquished, and much of it was bought by private hunting clubs because of the abundance of ducks and other waterfowl. The wetlands that are now publicly owned — Metzger Marsh, Ottawa Refuge and Magee Marsh — were purchased from these private concerns.

Metzger Marsh, which is used mostly for hunting and fishing, is accessed by Bono Road off Route 2. There is only one road through Metzger Marsh, running from the entrance all the way to its end at a fishing pier that juts into the lake. It parallels Wards Canal, just to the west, which empties into the lake next to the pier. There is a boat launch ramp on the canal, allowing protected access to the lake. A fishing channel east of the road yields crappies, channel catfish and spring bullheads. Most of the fishing, though, takes place off the pier, where anglers are likely to hook perch, catfish and freshwater drum, as well as white bass in early June.

Duck hunting is popular at Metzger Marsh, as it's located in a prime waterfowl area. Fall sees large numbers of mallards, black ducks and widgeons, and lesser populations of wood ducks, canvasbacks and others. In spring the area is visited by whistling swans. Herons, bitterns, cormorants and a wide variety of shorebirds are commonly spotted.

There are toilet facilities near the pier and ample parking along the road and at the pier. There are no trails at Metzger Marsh.

For more information contact the Ohio Department of Natural Resources, Division of Wildlife, 1840 Belcher Drive, Columbus, OH 43224-1329; 614-265-6300.

Ottawa National Wildlife Refuge

Located right next to Metzger Marsh is the 8,316-acre Ottawa National Wildlife Refuge. Even the drive into the refuge lets you know that something special is in store. During most months of the year, you can look out the car window on either side and see a dozen or so great egrets and a handful of great blue herons.

The refuge is comprised of five sites, though only the Ottawa site is open to the public. The other sites — West Sister Island, Cedar Point (not the amusement park, obviously), Darby and Navarre — are set aside for wildlife only. Eighty-two-acre West Sister Island is an important rookery for black-crowned herons, great blue herons and great egrets.

Ottawa Refuge is a bird-watcher's heaven. Nearly 300 bird species are regular visitors to the refuge, which is located on a branch of the Mississippi Flyway, a primary route for bird migration. Tundra swans, also known as whistling swans, arrive in the spring, along with the warblers. Bald eagles, nearly extinct in Ohio, nest in the refuge and can be seen year-round, though the best time to spot them is late winter through July when they are nesting or caring for their young. Pheasant, owls and hawks are commonly seen. Ducks, geese and other waterfowl are plentiful. In addition to the birds, many mammals inhabit the area. Muskrat are common, as are deer and rabbits. You may even see a mink or two.

Several trails wind throughout the refuge, following the ridges of man-made dikes above the wetland areas. Vistas stretch far in every direction, creating a spectacular visual impact. But because the area is so "wide open," wildlife is unlikely to be very close, making binoculars a necessity. There is little in the way of shade on the trails, so sunscreen is a must during spring and summer. Mosquitoes and other insects can be a problem; repellent is recommended. The trails are flat and easy to walk, and because they are elevated above the marsh they are usually dry.

The shortest of these trails is a quarter mile long, the longest four and a half miles. This, the Blue Trail, takes the visitor through the most varied habitats, including the eagles' nesting area and woodlands where spring warblers gather. A trail map and bird checklist is available at the kiosk by the parking lot.

The refuge is open dawn to sunset throughout the year. The office across from the parking lot is open during the week. Toilet facilities, which are free-standing affairs, are open at all times.

For more information contact the Refuge Manager, Ottawa National Wildlife Refuge Complex, 14000 W. State Route 2, Oak Harbor, OH 43449; 419-898-0014.

Magee Marsh State Wildlife Area

In 1951 the Ohio Division of Wildlife purchased 2,000-acre Magee Marsh from the Crane Creek Shooting Club, a private hunting club that could no longer afford its upkeep. Next to Ottawa National Wildlife Refuge, Magee Marsh is a small remaining part of the vast tract of wetlands edging the Great Black Swamp that for so many years stymied settlement in the area. A portion of the beach contained in the original parcel was later designated as Crane Creek State Park.

Like the Ottawa Refuge and Metzger Marsh to the west, Magee Marsh attracts large numbers of migratory songbirds and water-fowl, as well as supporting a permanent population of wildlife. Spring migration begins soon after the water begins to thaw, bringing large flocks of tundra swans and ducks. Spring is also a good time to see the bald eagles, peregrine falcons, osprey and hawks that frequent the marsh. Herons, egrets, ducks and geese are summer inhabitants. In the fall, thousands of Canada geese, mallards and other duck species crowd the marsh. Muskrats, mink, rabbits, skunks, raccoons, foxes and deer are common sights.

The first stop for visitors should be the Sportsmen's Migratory Bird Center on the entrance road that runs off from Route 2. In summer, it offers air-conditioned comfort while viewing the displays; in winter there's a cozy fireplace and sitting area. Displays include exhibits on the native inhabitants of the area, the lives of early settlers, history of the Great Black Swamp and hunting paraphernalia. There are tanks containing Lake Erie fish species and wetlands snakes and turtles, including snapping turtles. There is also a large display of mounted waterfowl and mammal

Nearly 300 species of birds have been identified at Sheldon Marsh.

specimens. The center is open year-round, 8 a.m. to 5 p.m., and noon to 6 p.m. on Saturday and Sunday during the spring and summer.

Crane Creek Wildlife Research Station, which is not open to the public, is housed on the second floor of the building. The station is responsible for developing and implementing effective wetlands management throughout Ohio. The many projects undertaken in recent years include reintroduction of river otters and beavers into Ohio waterways.

A short trail near the building leads over a boardwalk to a 42-foot-high observation deck. Farther down the road, opposite the beach at Crane Creek State Park, is the Magee Marsh Bird Trail, a 1.2 mile round trip. The trail is built entirely on a boardwalk, making it wheelchair and stroller accessible. And the fact that it is above the marshy ground makes it especially attractive for spring bird watchers who usually find themselves slogging through mud in their pursuit of feathered friends. The Bird Trail is a favorite haunt of mosquitoes, however, so be prepared. A

Hiking and wildlife observation at Sheldon Marsh.

third trail leads over a beachfront dike east of the Crane Creek beach. Hiking is allowed, but no swimming or picnicking is permitted.

Early October through early December is hunting season at Magee Marsh, so restricted hours are apt to be in effect. If you plan to visit during these times, call ahead to get current information. Hunting is allowed only for those holding permits, which must be applied for.

For more information contact the Magee Marsh Wildlife Area, 13229 West State Route 2, Oak Harbor, OH 43449; 419-898-0960.

Crane Creek State Park

Named for the creek that flows into the lake west of the park, Crane Creek's big attraction is its beach. There is a park office located at the entrance just off Route 2, but from there you must drive through Magee Marsh to get to the rest of Crane Creek, and many are confused by the close proximity of the two.

The beach is among the most beautiful on the lake — three-quarters of a mile long and 300 feet wide, shaded by tall cottonwoods. There are picnic tables, grills and a picnic shelter. Rest rooms and changing rooms are nearby. The water tends to be calm here, and with its gradually sloping bottom, this beach is a good one for children. Visitors may want to take advantage of the adjacent boardwalk trail, one of the best birding spots on the state, or the beach trail just to the east.

For information contact the park office at 419-898-2495.

Catawba Island State Park

This 18-acre park is a bit hard to find. Head toward Marblehead on Route 163, then north on Route 53. Turn west onto West Catawba Road, drive five miles to Moores Dock Road, then turn left. The entrance is shortly thereafter. The park, which is for day use only, has a fishing pier, a launch ramp, a shaded grassy picnic area with grills and tables, and 200-vehicle parking lot. Not surprisingly, the park is used primarily by fishermen who come to try their luck in the "Walleye Capital of the World."

For more information call 419-797-4530.

East Harbor State Park

At the fringe of what was once the Great Black Swamp, East Harbor sits on a peninsula that juts into the lake just west of Lakeside. The park is most popular with campers, fishermen and boaters. There are 570 campsites, 366 of them with electricity. At the marina, there's a restaurant, store and room for 123 seasonal boats. Entering the park, you'll first come upon the campground and a nature center, which offers programs and guided hikes. The land narrows as the road passes by East Harbor, to the right, and Middle Harbor, to the left. These protected, marshy areas offer shelter to large populations of ducks, geese, ducks and terns, as well as frogs, toads and water snakes. Great blue herons, egrets and black-crowned night herons are

The beach at Crane Creek State Park.

regular visitors. During the spring migration, warblers and other songbirds make East Harbor their stop before the long flight across the lake. The road ends at the beach — 1,500 feet of sandy shoreline. The marina has a separate entrance to the west of the campground and beach entrance, at the edge of West Harbor. The park has seven miles of hiking trails, but during periods of high lake levels large sections of them are likely to be underwater, or at least quite wet.

For more information contact the park office at 419-734-4424 or the camp office at 419-734-5857.

Sheldon Marsh State Nature Preserve

Stop at Sheldon Marsh on any mild day in early spring and you'll find it swarming. Not with bees, bugs or any other many-legged creatures, but with bird watchers. This 463-acre preserve, located on U.S. Route 6 between Sandusky and Huron, is one of the prime locations on the south shore of the lake for migrating birds to stop in the spring and fall. Warblers, tanagers, finches and orioles are common visitors to the forests and marshy areas of the preserve.

The gates at the entrance to the preserve once marked the beginning of the road to Cedar Point, farther west. The road, which ran out over a barrier beach, was constantly being washed away by the lake, and after many years of frustration caused by this natural event the entrance to the amusement park was moved to its present location.

The preserve is named for Dr. Dean Sheldon, a conservation-minded physician from Sandusky who owned 56 acres of the land in the 1950s. He introduced plant species that provided food for the bird population and built nest boxes for bluebirds and kestrels. When the Ohio Department of Natural Resources purchased the land in 1979, it was combined with a 330-acre parcel and dedicated as Sheldon Marsh State Nature Preserve. It is the largest remaining undeveloped section of the Sandusky Bay area, and as such is an important shoreline habitat.

In addition to the nearly 300 species of birds that frequent the preserve, there are eastern fox snakes, northern water snakes, painted turtles, Blanding's turtles, raccoons, groundhogs, muskrats and foxes. A variety of wildflowers also flourish here, including the magnificent cardinal flower, whose scarlet spiked flowers bloom in the summer.

The "trail" that leads from the parking lot out to the lake is actually the original paved roadway to Cedar Point. A couple of short paths through the woods branch off from the main trail, and though these offer good opportunities to spot hard-to-see birds, they can be quite muddy during the spring. About halfway along the trail there is an observation deck that looks out over the marsh formed by the barrier beach. This is a good place to see egrets, herons and other waterfowl. The trail continues to the lake shore and ends at a NASA pump station. Walking out along the barrier beach is not allowed due to its delicate nature.

As at all Ohio State Nature Preserves, hunting, swimming, picnicking and the collection of plants or animals are forbidden.

For more information contact the Division of Natural Areas and Preserves at 614-265-6453.

Old Woman Creek State Nature Preserve

Pay close attention as you travel on Route 6 east of Huron or you will miss Old Woman Creek entirely. The narrow creek that passes under the road gives no hint that, just to the south, it forms a wide, lake-like body of water that supports a rich variety of life.

Old Woman Creek is a 571-acre nature preserve and site of the Ohio Center for Coastal Wetlands Studies. It is also one of 22 National Estuarine Research Reserves, protected by the federal government and administered by the National Oceanic and Atmospheric Administration (NOAA), and the only fresh water estuary among them. The area includes marshland, a 15-acre island, a barrier beach, oak-hickory forests, old crop fields, and one of the finest remaining examples of an estuary on the Great Lakes.

Estuaries are generally thought to be places where fresh and salt water mix and where water levels are affected by tides. Even though the lake is only slightly affected by lunar tidal pull, water levels are subject to changes due to weather. And while salinity is not a factor here, the chemical composition of the creek water is very different from that of the lake. When the creek water mixes with lake water, a third chemical composition results. This third type of water supports different species than either the creek or the lake, making the area unique.

The waters of the estuary serve as a spawning ground for a number of species including largemouth bass, sunfish, shiners, perch, crappie and brown bullhead. Cattails, American water lotus and white water lilies thrive in the rich environment, along with the ducks, herons, geese, egrets and shorebirds that find an abundance of food here.

Nearly 300 species of birds have been spotted at Old Woman Creek. The population swells in the spring and fall, as migrating birds stop to rest before or after journeying across the lake. Warblers, finches, vireos and hummingbirds are regulars. Bald eagles nest here and occasionally tundra swans are seen. Other inhabitants include spotted turtles, eastern fox snakes and foxes.

The area around the estuary has supported human life from approximately 11,000 years ago when Paleo-Indian hunters roamed the Great Lakes region. Spear points found during excavations in the summers of 1976 and 1977 are estimated to be about 9,200 years old. It wasn't until far later that Indians settled into villages and began to grow crops. Evidence found along Old Woman Creek has led archeologists to believe that it was the site of a village during the late 15th century. Carbonized corn kernels found here indicate that the inhabitants farmed corn, but scientists believe that most of their food came from hunting, gathering, or fishing the rich waters of the estuary and Lake Erie.

The name "Old Woman's Creek" has its origins in a Huron legend that tells of a young Indian woman, Wintasta, who was killed while trying to save her white lover from execution. Wintasta's mother, Minehonto, was so distraught by her daughter's death that she drowned herself in the creek the following night. The creek was named by white settlers who had heard the tale.

Much can be learned about the Indian inhabitants and their way of life at the Visitor Center on the south side of Route 6. Displays also illuminate the natural history of the area and include aquariums with local fish and turtles.

Two short trails wind through the reserve. The Edward Walper Trail, named for the farmer who sold his land to the state in 1978, begins at the Visitor Center and passes through meadows and woods before leading to an observation deck overlooking the wide water of the estuary. In the middle sits Star Island, a 15-acre forested island that was once the location of a vineyard. It is now inaccessible. The trail loops back to the Visitor Center.

The Wintasta Trail, another loop, branches off from and returns to the Edward Walper Trail. It leads through both scrub and forest, climbing and descending with the terrain. Part of it is covered by boardwalk but much is not. Portions of the trail are likely so be wet and muddy, so hiking boots are recommended.

There is another parking lot on the north side of Route 6 that gives access to the barrier beach.

The Visitor Center is open Wednesday through Sunday most of the year; however, in January, February and March it is open Monday through Friday, but closed on the weekends. The trails are open daily April through December; weekdays only the rest of the year.

For more information contact the reserve at 419-433-4601.

DIVERSIONS

Milan

South of Sandusky on U.S. Route 250 is the town of Milan. Although it is miles inland from the lake, Milan was once a bustling port. In 1839 a canal was built that linked it to the Huron River, thus also to the lake, and the town did a booming trade shipping local grain and other products. When railroads were found to be more expedient than canals, business fell flat, and after a flood damaged the canal it was never repaired. Milan became a sleepy little town.

But this quiet hamlet produced a famous son — Thomas Alva Edison. You can tour his modest home and the adjacent museum at the Edison Birthplace Museum (419-499-2135). The museum is closed in January; hours vary the rest of the year so call for information. There's more local history to be learned at the Milan Historical Museum (419-499-2968), where you'll find a complex that includes a blacksmith shop, country store, and the Galpin

House, which houses an art glass collection and exhibit of 400 dolls. Milan is also known for its fine examples of Greek Revival architecture and for its antiques shops. Contact the Milan Chamber of Commerce at PO Box 544, Milan, OH 44846; 419-499-2100.

Fremont

Follow U.S. 6 southwest out of Sandusky and you'll come to Fremont, home of the Rutherford B. Hayes Presidential Center (419-332-2081). Hayes, 19th President of the United States, resided in Fremont at the family estate, "Spiegel Grove," before and after his presidential term. The 19th-century mansion, furnished with antiques, is on the grounds of the center and is open to visitors. Also on the grounds are a museum and the first presidential library in the U.S. The estate covers 25 acres, much of it wooded.

Avon Lake/Avon

A drive south from the lake on Route 83 about 10 miles east of Lorain is worth the time and effort. You'll come first to Avon Lake, where two small, family-owned wineries produce some very nice wines unavailable anywhere else. The wines of the John Christ Winery (32421 Walker Road; 440-933-9672) have won many awards, including their Cayuga, which won the 1996 Gold Medal at the Ohio Wine Producers Competition.

The Christ Winery produces the gamut, from dry Chardonnays and Seyval Blanc, to Pink Catawba and Niagara. There are also fruit wines available. Wine can be tasted and purchased during business hours, but the place really comes alive on Friday and Saturday nights when the adjacent tasting room is open.

The Klingshirn Winery (33050 Webber Road; 440-933-6666) has been in the wine business since 1935, with the third generation of Klingshirns now at the helm. They make a wide variety of still and sparkling wines, growing most of the grapes themselves. While they have traditionally concentrated on Labrusca and hybrids, they are expanding their offerings to include Vinifera.

Farther south, Route 83 takes you to Route 254. Follow 254 west and you'll arrive at the town of Avon and the French Creek Antique District. This area has more than 30 antique and craft shops concentrated in a few blocks. There's also a country store, a greenhouse, coffee house and several restaurants.

WHAT ABOUT MICHIGAN?

There are approximately 30 miles of Lake Erie shoreline in Michigan, most of it the unattractive urban sprawl of Detroit and therefore beyond the realm of this guide. The industrial town of Monroe, however, has some things worth dropping by

FOR THE SPORTS ENTHUSIAST

Some of Lake Erie's best water sport activities are found along Ohio's western shoreline and the islands of the western basin. Here's what you'll find:

Scuba - Over the years, the lake's bad temper has sent hundreds of ships to its bottom. Many of them are scattered around the islands in the western basin. The hitch? You need a boat to get to them. No problem. There are several dive charters that specialize in local shipwrecks. For more information contact Adventures in Diving (440-572-2005), New Wave Dive Shop (419-734-2240), North Coast Scuba (419-798-5557) or Dale's Diving Shop (419-625-4134).

Fishing charters - It's not called "Walleye Capital of the World" for nothing. The western basin of Lake Erie, with its shallow water, rocky shoals and warm temperature is the perfect spawning ground for yellow perch, small-mouth bass, largemouth bass, white perch, steelhead trout and the legendary walleye. The area is popular with fisher men all year, but especially March through July. The Sandusky

Charter Boat Association (1-800-338-2785) can arrange a charter that meets your needs.

Windsurfing - You don't have to be in Hawaii to skim over the water's surface with the wind. North Coast Windsurfing in Vermilion (440-967-3493) will teach you how. They guarantee that you'll learn how to windsurf in one three-hour lesson. Lessons are available mornings or afternoons seven days a week. Family lessons are also available.

Parasailing - If your idea of a water sport doesn't actually involve getting wet, parasailing may be for you. Put-in-Bay Parasailing (419-285-3703) will put you 500 feet up in the air and bring you back down again without a splash. Then you can buy one of their "I DID IT!" T-shirts and impress all your friends. Reservations are recommended.

Sail charters - The Red Witch (419-798-1244), a 77-foot topsail schooner based in Port Clinton, sails to the Lake Erie Islands, to Cleveland, and to a variety of other destinations April through October. Group, corporate and private charters are available.

Sea kayaking - Lake Erie Sea Kayak Adventures (216-283-8500 or 440-209-0312) offers two-day kayaking and camping trips from Catawba Island to Kelleys Island. Trips are open to adults and children 12 and over (children under 18 must be accompanied by an adult). Participants must demonstrate proficiency in sea kayaking or must take an introductory three-hour course.

for. Located about 15 miles north of Toledo, Ohio, Monroe is one of the oldest towns in Michigan. It was founded in 1780 by French settlers and was first called Frenchtown. In 1813, it was the site of the River Raisin Massacre, one of the bloodiest battles of the War of 1812. The River Raisin Battlefield Visitor Center (1403 Elm Street; 313-243-7136 or 313-243-7137) has displays, maps and a diorama depicting the battle and other aspects of the war.

Monroe's biggest claim to fame, though, may be that it was once the home of Gen. George Custer. You can see him captured in bronze at the corner of N. Monroe Street and W. Elm Avenue. To learn about his family and life stop by the Monroe County Historical Museum (126 S. Monroe Street; 313-243-7137).

Just north of Monroe is Sterling State Park (2800 State Park Road; 313-289-2715), Michigan's only state park on Lake Erie. There are facilities for camping, fishing and swimming, as well as interpretive programs given by the park staff. The marshes and lagoons are great places to spot birds and other wildlife.

N
W — E
S

5 miles

Pelee
Island

⑨

⑥
⑦

⑧

North Bass
Island (privately owned)

Middle Bass Island

③

LAKE ERIE

South Bass
Island

② ①

⑤
Kelleys Island
④

1. Put-in-Bay
2. South Bass Island State Park
3. Lonz Winery
4. Ferry dock and town
5. Kelleys Island State Park
6. West Dock
7. Pelee Island Wine Pavilion
8. Fish Point Provincial Nature Reserve
9. Lighthouse Point Provincial Nature Reserve

Chapter Two

Islands
A Vacationer's Delight

From the air, the 20 islands strewn over the western basin of Lake Erie look like mossy green mounds rising from the surrounding water. Most of them are small, too small to have a village, though some have been inhabited by the odd anti-social character or two over the years. They have names like Mouse Island, Starve Island, Ballast Island, Sugar Island or Rattlesnake Island, most of which have some significance.

Ballast Island, a 10-acre pile of limestone, was where Commodore Oliver Hazard Perry picked up the ballast for his famous Lake Erie fleet during the War of 1812. Starve Island is so-named for the skeleton found on the tiny two-acre plot; legend has it that the unlucky fellow starved to death. Rattlesnake Island was named for the venomous reptiles that once overran it. Mouse Island seems to have been just small.

Long before the islands saw white men, they were occupied by Indians. These first inhabitants had vanished by the time settlers from the East arrived, but they left behind traces of their existence. The most impressive is Inscription Rock on Kelleys Island. Though now worn by centuries of weather and curious visitors, the large, smooth-faced limestone slab is engraved with over a hundred inscriptions of birds, animals and human figures. There have been many theories about the meaning of the inscriptions — that they depict the story of the Erie Indians, that they were carved by the Mound Builders — but there is no definitive answer to the mystery. Archeologists believe the carvings were made sometime in the early 1600s.

Other artifacts were discovered, especially on Kelleys Island, including tomahawks, arrowheads, grindstones, pottery and fishhooks. Burial grounds also have been unearthed; one on South Bass Island contained the skeleton of a seven-foot-tall man.

The islands were slow to be settled, isolated as they were and difficult to get to much of the year. After the War of 1812 they were divided between Canada and the United States, with Canada receiving the largest of the lot, Pelee Island, and a handful of small islands. What were later to become Kelleys Island and the Bass Islands went to the United States, along with a scattering of small, uninhabitable islands.

The American islands were part of the Firelands, land set aside for the benefit of Connecticut residents who had been burned out by the British during the Revolutionary War. But the islands were largely ignored. Settlers flocked instead to Sandusky, Port Clinton and Huron. Things remained quiet on the islands until curiosity got the better of the lake mariners who sailed regularly back and forth past these green havens. They began to drop anchor and explore the places. Talk of the islands' appeal spread.

There were rich cedar forests, which would eventually be chopped and used to fuel the engines of the first lake steamers. Limestone for quarrying and building was abundant, especially on Kelleys Island. The land was suitable for crops, and would soon be found perfect for grape growing.

Gradually, settlements grew on Kelleys Island and the Bass Islands. Italians, Slavs, Hungarians, Greeks, Germans and other Europeans came to work the quarries. German immigrants brought their wine-making skills to the Bass Islands, although it was as a tourist spot that South Bass would later gain fame. Canada's Pelee Island was slow to develop until its malarial swamps were drained for farmland. The smaller islands remained uninhabited, except for those on which a lighthouse had been built.

PEDALING THE ISLANDS

The islands offer some of the best cycling anywhere on the lake. Here are some helpful things to know:

SOUTH BASS ISLAND has numerous bike rentals and good paved roads. An especially scenic route runs along the lake on West Shore Road, where cottages and private homes are set back into the woods opposite the water. South Bass, however, has the most traffic of any of the islands, a consideration for families with small children.

MIDDLE BASS ISLAND, like South Bass, has good roads and bike rentals. It is an excellent place to bike since there is little traffic, though it is the smallest of the islands and therefore has fewer miles of roads to explore.

KELLEYS ISLAND also has bike rentals and plenty of miles of paved roads, though many of the side roads are made of coarse gravel unsuitable for riding. Unfortunately, there is not a road that circles the entire perimeter of the island, but pretty Lakeshore Road runs along approximately half of it.

PELEE ISLAND has many enthusiastic supporters among cyclists — and just as many detractors. What you think of it depends largely on what you expect. Most of the roads are not paved, but they are fine gravel easily negotiated by bikes. Be prepared for plenty of dust if there hasn't been recent rain, and mud if there has been. The two paved roads, West Shore Road and East-West Road, have good surfaces. West Shore Road is particularly scenic. It is possible to ride the whole perimeter of the island, though most of it is gravel. Mountain or hybrid bikes do especially well on these roads. One of the big advantages for families is that there's very little traffic. Bike rentals are available.

Twenty-acre Green Island was one such island. It has been home only for a lighthouse keeper and his family over the years, a lonely existence that wasn't without its dangers. New Year's Eve 1863 was a case in point. It had been unseasonably warm, with balmy breezes that hovered around 60 degrees. Then one of

The "world's longest bar" on Put-in-Bay.

Lake Erie's characteristically sudden and fierce storms rolled in, dropping the temperature to -25 in an hour's time. In the midst of the storm the lighthouse went up in flames. The fire, visible from nearby South Bass Island, alarmed spectators but there was no way to get to lighthouse keeper Colonel Drake and his family. The Drakes tried heroically to put the fire out, but it was hopeless. When Drake realized all was lost and that he and his family were likely to freeze to death in the driving storm, he plunged into the burning building and salvaged a mattress. The Drakes huddled under the mattress until the next day, when rescuers made their way gingerly across the thin ice using planks and brought the Drakes to safety on South Bass.

Nearly a hundred years after settlement, the establishment of regular air service among the islands and to the mainland helped relieve the islands of their isolation. In 1929, Milton Hershberger piloted the first plane to ever land on South Bass. It was such a momentous event that children were dismissed from school so they could watch it. Shortly after, Hershberger began Erie Isle Airways, which eventually connected the Bass Islands and Kelleys Island to Port Clinton. His preferred plane was the Ford Tri-Motor, known around the islands as the Tin Goose.

A Tin Goose had three engines, one on the nose, the other two under each wing. The metal planes were stout and awkward-looking but they did the job. They could fly on one engine if they had to and could haul cargo and as many as 20 passengers. The Tin Goose (there were seven of them in service at one point) carried mail, supplies, passengers and sometimes even bodies. It served as a school bus, carrying children from the smaller islands to Put-in-Bay to attend classes. Eventually Hershberger sold his business, but the Tin Goose continued to fly for many years. Long after it was replaced by newer planes for the cargo and passenger runs, it continued to take tourists up for aerial tours of the islands. Today, Griffing Flying Service serves the islands in much the same way Erie Isle Airways did earlier.

To one degree or another, all the major islands do some kind of tourist trade. All are visited by ferries from the mainland daily during the spring, summer and fall months. South Bass, also known by its town's name, Put-in-Bay, is the busiest with its restaurants, bars and beautiful waterfront park. Across a narrow strip of water, Middle Bass draws visitors to Lonz Winery. Kelleys Island, though quieter than South Bass, has several bed and breakfasts, a winery and a state park. Pelee, the most rural of them all, attracts nature lovers, solitude seekers, and increasingly, people who come to sample the excellent island wines.

PLACES
South Bass Island

It doesn't take much of an excuse to have fun on South Bass, or Put-in-Bay, as it's better known. (Put-in-Bay is actually the name of the island's one town, but has come to refer to the entire island). Fun is built right into the place, from its rental bicycles, golf carts and antique cars to its fudge shops and ice cream stands. Put-in-Bay is also home of the world's longest bar, or so the owner claims. In the summer, visiting boats are tied off to one another ten-deep in the harbor, and dozens of ferries a day deposit hundreds of visitors onto this 1,450-acre playground.

Aside from its lively watering holes and restaurants, South Bass is perhaps best known for the 352-foot monument that dominates the island, Perry's Victory and International Peace Memorial. Built from 1912 to 1915 of pink Massachusetts granite, the monument honors the British and American sailors who lost their lives in the Battle of Lake Erie during the War of 1812.

In the summer of 1813, Commodore Perry chose the harbor at Put-in-Bay on South Bass to wait out the British, who were holed up in Fort Malden to the west and quickly running out of supplies. By September 10, Captain R.H. Barclay, the officer in charge of the British fleet, was desperate. It was either fight or starve, and he chose the former. He pulled his fleet out and prepared to face Perry.

It looked as though it would be an easy victory for the British. Five minutes into the battle, before the Americans aboard their flagship, the Lawrence, could even get their guns firing, the British blew a hole through the side of the ship. It withstood hit after hit, until Perry had to abandon it. Eighty-three out of 103 men had been killed or wounded. Dodging shots, Perry lowered a boat from the Lawrence and rowed to the Niagara, another of his fleet.

But Barclay's flagship, the Detroit, had also sustained damage. Once Perry established himself on the Niagara and opened fire, it took only 10 minutes to finish off the Detroit. Barclay delivered his surrender to a weary but victorious Perry. The dead sailors were buried off Middle Sister Island, to the northwest; the captured fleet was taken to Put-in-Bay, where the wounded were cared for and the dead officers honored with ceremonies. It was when he reported to his superior, General William Henry Harrison, that Perry penned the now-famous words, "We have met the enemy and they are ours."

In 1854, South Bass, along with Middle Bass, North Bass, Gibraltar and Sugar Islands, was bought by J. D. Rivera, a wealthy New York businessman. He divided South Bass into

The Allan Herschell carousel on Put-in-Bay.

plots and sold them at a good price. The settlers began arriving, particularly Germans who came to grow grapes and make wine. Shortly thereafter the island was discovered by tourists. Many guest houses and hotels sprang up over the next half-century, but none was grander than the Hotel Victory.

When it was completed in 1892, the Hotel Victory was advertised as the largest resort in the world. The dining room sat 1,200. The adjoining lobby could accommodate up to a thousand people who gathered daily to listen to a live orchestra. Outside, 21 acres of gardens sprawled across the shoreline where boathouses and beaches awaited the pampered guests. There were sumptuous appointments, luxury at every turn and hundreds of staff waiting to fill every need. Then it all ended one night in 1919 when the hotel went up in flames and burned to the ground. Today there's nothing left of the huge resort except the foundation of the swimming pool, which can still be found in the woods at the state park on the island's west side.

A few of the island's righteous citizens may have thought it was

The Round House Bar on Put-in-Bay.

just punishment, for the tourist business — especially the Sunday excursion boats — was frowned upon by church-goers. Jay Cooke, son of the well known Sandusky lawyer, Eleutheros Cooke, was one of them. Cooke had bought Gibraltar island, just a stone's throw away from the harbor at South Bass, and built a 15-room Victorian mansion there. It pained him to see the Sunday revelers breaking the Sabbath, and he became a vocal opponent of the island's goings-on, particularly the drinking, and particularly on Sundays. He fought a losing battle, though, for neither the visitors nor the lively German settlers were willing to give up their beer — and certainly not on Sundays, their day of rest.

And so Put-in-Bay's reputation as a fun-loving, beer-chugging island was born. Fifty years later, Harlan Hatcher, in his definitive history of Lake Erie, called Put-in-Bay "frowsy and vulgar with its cheap entertainment joints for excursionists and its dilapidated hotels." Fortunately, things have changed. It's still fun-loving, and you can still find plenty of bars, but you will also find an antique merry-go-round, a geode you can walk into,

The beach at Kelleys Island State Park.

beaches, charming bed and breakfasts, quiet tree-lined roads, and the only Alaskan Birdhouse Museum in the lower forty-eight.

Most of the action takes place in the town. It's situated on the north side of the island on a bay facing Middle Bass, just a long stone's throw away. Victorian buildings housing restaurants, shops and bars line one side of the main street, Delaware Avenue, while the other is occupied by the grassy, shady expanse of De Rivera Park, named for the island's owner in the mid-1800s, who donated the land for the park. There are benches, playground facilities, and picnic tables. Public rest rooms and showers are available in a new building at the east end of the park.

If you go to Put-in-Bay with young children, you won't get them past Kimberly's Carousel without taking a ride. Located downtown, this Allan Herschell carousel was built in North Tonawanda, New York, in 1917. It's one of the last of its kind — with all wooden animals — still in operation. Historic scenes of the island, including the old Hotel Victory and Tin Goose, are painted on the crown.

Much of the island's past has been preserved in the buildings along Delaware Avenue. Just east of the park on the same side of the street is the old Schlitz Ice House, which is now a gift shop. At the turn of the century it served as a storage building for ice cut from the lake in the winter. Its sawdust-filled walls provided insulation that kept the ice frozen well into the summer months.

Across the street and to the west is the Crescent Tavern, built in 1871. The building was previously a hotel, at one time owned by Edith Brown Alexander, granddaughter of the famous abolitionist John Brown, and her husband. Farther west is the Round House, build by "Round House" Smith. The building, which measures 150 feet in circumference, has always been a restaurant or bar. Next door is the Park Hotel, also built by Smith. Constructed in 1873, it is one of the oldest continuously operating hotels in Ohio. It is noted for the etched glass windows in the lobby.

Down the street and around the corner on Catawba Avenue is the Town Hall. Built in 1887, it is one of the few buildings on the Bass Islands built of brick. Next door is a building that served as a store and service station when it was built in 1911. Today it houses the Lake Erie Islands Historical Society Museum (419-285-2804), which displays island memorabilia and artifacts. The museum and gift shop are open daily 11 a.m. - 5 p.m. May, June and September; 10 a.m. - 6 p.m. July and August.

If you continue west along the waterfront on Bayview Avenue you will pass the old Doller Villa. Built by wealthy entrepreneur Valentine Dollar about 1870, it's an impressive sight with its octagonal corner tower. Farther east are the Crew's Nest, a private club, and the Put-in-Bay Yacht Club.

The road winds past tiny Oak Point State Park, a one-acre plot with public docks for day or overnight use.

Just beyond the park is the Aquatic Resource Center (419-285-3701) operated by the Ohio Department of Natural Resources,

A dock on Kelleys Island.

Division of Wildlife. Until 1988 it served as a working fish hatchery. It then became a visitors' center focusing on the marine life of Lake Erie. In 1994 it closed, and remained so until the summer of 1997, when it reopened as a education center, again focusing on marine life. Large freshwater tanks display many of the native fishes of the lake, and staff are available to answer questions. More exhibits are planned for the future.

Looking toward Gibraltar Island just offshore, you can see the Franz Theodore Stone Laboratory, operated by Ohio State University. The island was donated to the school by its second owner, Julius Stone, who stipulated that the laboratory be named for his father, Franz Theodore. It serves as a field station for biological studies, and is one of the oldest fresh water field stations in the country. Every summer university and high school students and teachers study at the laboratory. Jay Cooke's mansion, also owned by the university, is at Gibraltar's eastern tip. The island is not open to tourists.

On the other side of the downtown area, the 352-foot Perry's

Victory and International Peace Memorial (419-285-2184) towers over the east side of the island. Dedicated September 10, 1913, on the 100th anniversary of the Battle of Lake Erie, it is one of the largest such monuments in the world. At the time of its dedication the bodies of the three British and three American officers were removed from their previous burial site and interred under the floor of the memorial.

The monument is intended, not just as a memorial to those who lost their lives in the famous battle, but as a tribute to the lasting peace between two neighboring countries. It is administered by the National Park Service and is open to visitors daily from late April to early October.

There is an observation deck near the top of the monument that affords a spectacular view of the other islands and surrounding lake. Visitors must climb narrow, winding stairs part of the way; the rest is by elevator.

A sandy beach close to the monument is a popular place for sunning and swimming.

Several inland attractions draw a steady stream of visitors during the summer months. One of the most popular is Heineman Winery and Crystal Cave (419-285-2811). The winery has been in continuous operation by the Heineman family since its founding in 1888. Although wineries flourished on South Bass before Prohibition, Heineman's is the only to survive that setback (largely due to the sale of grape juice accompanied by instructions on how to make "vinegar"). The winery produces several hundred cases annually, most of which is consumed on the premises in the winery's tasting room and garden.

Beneath the winery is the Crystal Cave, discovered in 1897 when Gustav Heineman's workers were digging a well on his property. The cave, lined with bluish-white celestite crystals, is actually the largest known geode in the world. Tours offered May through September include the winery, cave and a glass of wine or grape juice.

Across the street is another attraction, Perry's Cave (419-285-

2405). It was supposedly discovered by Perry in 1813 and used to house both prisoners and supplies during the war. It is encrusted with stalactites and stalagmites, although many have been broken off over the years by visitors wanting to take a piece of the cave home with them. The cave also contains a small lake of crystal clear water which is somehow connected to Lake Erie, since its level rises and falls with that of the lake. There are guided tours daily during the summer months.

Half the fun of going to the Alaskan Birdhouse Wildlife Museum (419-285-2141) is talking with the owners. Veterans of many years living in Alaska, they have lots of tales to tell. Children especially will be fascinated by stories about the 200 or so game birds, waterfowl, mammals and fish displayed in their natural habitats. The museum is located on Meechen Road on the island's west side.

Older children and adults will enjoy Stonehenge (419-285-2585), a historic home tour and gift shop. Located on Langram Road east of the airport, Stonehenge is a 19th-century stone house that belonged to a wine-producing family. An oasis of quiet on a very busy island, it sits on seven acres of woods and landscaped grounds that include a wine press cottage. Visitors take a self-guided tour through the house and grounds, aided by an audio recording. The gift shop adjacent to the house is one of the nicest on the island, with its selection of nautical items and collectibles.

For a narrated tour of the island, hop on the Tour Train at its downtown depot. It stops at the Heineman Winery and Crystal Cave, Perry's Memorial and the Alaskan Wildlife Museum. For more information and rates contact Island Transportation, Inc. at 419-285-4855.

Far from the hustle of downtown, South Bass Island State Park (419-285-2112 or 419-797-4530) on a bay at the island's western end, offers a quiet alternative. There is a launching ramp and fishing pier, but no mooring facility. A wide grassy area with a swing set and slides is a nice place to picnic. The beach is not sand, but made up of large water-smoothed rocks. Because of the rocky bottom and the protection of the bay, the water here is often very clear, making it a good place to snorkel. Care must be

Rain doesn't dampen spirits of cyclists on Pelee Island.

taken, however, to avoid boats and the Jet Skis that are rented near the boat ramp.

The park has a large campground area, high on a wooded bluff overlooking the lake. The ruins of the Hotel Victory swimming pool can be found in this area. Closer to the pier there are also four "cabents," a sort of cross between a cabin and a tent. These wooden structures with fabric roofs serve as efficiency-type accommodations, with sleeping room for six; a kitchen area including stove, sink and fridge; a central eating area; and a bathroom with shower. Rentals are by the week only. These are very popular, and a lottery system has been established for their rental. Applications must be received by January 31 for the summer season. For information and application forms contact Lake Erie Islands State Parks, 4049 E. Moore's Dock Road, Port Clinton, OH 43452; phone 419-797-4530.

Where to stay:

There are so many options for accommodations on Put-in-Bay

that this guide can't begin to cover them all. Instead, here is a selection of places that meet a variety of needs, each special in its own way. But be forewarned — Put-in-Bay is one of the most expensive places on the entire lake to catch a night's sleep. Many accommodations have variable rates dependent on the day of week or time of season. Some require two-night's stay on weekends; cottages generally require a full-week's booking. Most are open only seasonally.

Park Hotel
PO Box 60
Put-in-Bay, OH 43456
419-285-3581

This is the island's only hotel, built in the 1870s. The scene outside is dubious — a smoky haze from outdoor grills, the heavy aroma of barbecue, and picnic tables full of chowing-down, beer-guzzling tourists. But take a step inside the Park, and it's the very picture of Victorian gentility. The lobby's only concession to modernity is a television. The second and third floors are occupied by 25 guest rooms that were originally segregated into men's quarters and women's quarters. They are comfortable and nicely decorated but simple. The rooms have ceiling fans, although the hotel is air-conditioned. True to 19th century tradition, the bathrooms are shared.

Ashley's Island House
557 Catawba Ave.
PO Box 395
Put-in-Bay, OH 43456
419-285-2844

Close enough to town to walk to the many shops and restaurants, but far enough to be away from the crowds, Ashley's is a 12-room inn charmingly decorated in country antiques. The house was built in 1863 by George Gascoyne, a prominent island builder. In 1900 it was converted into a boarding house for visiting ship's officers. Three of the rooms have private baths; others are shared. There is a two-bedroom suite with bath. The owners prefer adult guests.

Buck & Ollie's Bed & Breakfast
425 Loraine Avenue
PO Box 342
Put-in-Bay, OH 43456
419-285-2529 (summer)
419-447-5448 (winter)

No, Buck and Ollie aren't the owners — they're the dogs. The real owners are Dale and Kathy McKee, proud proprietors of a newly opened B & B. Located in a quiet residential neighborhood close to downtown, their home is spacious and modern. (In 1996, says Kathy, they "added a house onto a cottage.") There are four guest rooms — two rooms with two queen beds and two rooms with one queen bed. Children are welcome. A spacious deck with wicker furniture offers a nice place to enjoy the continental breakfast.

The A-frame in Winsome Wood
700 Columbus Ave. (Reservations)
Put-in-Bay, OH 43456
419-285-6138 (summer)
419-448-4509 (winter)

This lovely A-frame house on quiet, wooded Meechen Road is the perfect place for a large family or two families wishing to share a vacation. The house sleeps 10 in three queen beds, one king and two twins. The main area includes a living room, dining room and kitchen with a cathedral ceiling and a fireplace overlooking a furnished wrap-around deck. There are two bedrooms off the living area, one with a fireplace, and a loft above. The house has two full baths and what is probably the only bidet on the island. The selling point for children, though, is the large tree house and sandbox located in the backyard.

Wisteria Inn
1331 Langram Road
Put-in-Bay, OH 43456
419-285-2828 or
216-221-4435

This charming B & B is the old Alois Niele House, built in 1860. Its location across from the airport overlooking the lake makes it an attractive place for those who wish to be away from the bustle of downtown. The house was one of the first brick structures on the island; the bricks were hauled from the mainland over the ice during a cold winter. There are five rooms and two baths in the main house, all beautifully decorated. The large breakfast room overlooks the yard. For small families, there's another building called "the loft," which has a queen-size bed and two singles, with a private lake view deck. The Wisteria Inn offers some of the best B & B rates on the island.

South Shore Beach Resort
PO Box 205
Put-in-Bay, OH 43456
419-285-4321

For those who prefer condo-type accommodations, South Shore may be the place. There are eight two-bedroom units, all perched at the edge of the lake near the airport off Langram Road. Each suite has a fully equipped kitchen, two full baths, a washer and dryer, TV with VCR, and a telephone. They can accommodate up to six people. There is daily maid and linen service. An in-ground pool, gas grills and picnic tables are also on the grounds. These are new, beautifully decorated units — and they are priced accordingly.

Where to eat:

Put-in-Bay has yet to see the arrival of fine dining. Food is generally high priced and much of it is just a notch above standard burger and fries fare. But forget about the food — you went for the fun, right? Just in case hunger strikes, here are a couple of places that offer better-than-average eats.

Crescent Tavern
Delaware Ave.
419-285-4211

Right in the middle of downtown, the historic Crescent Tavern, while certainly not staid, is one of the quieter eating establishments cum bar on the island. It's actually four places in one. There's an indoor bar, a full service dining room, an outdoor bar with live entertainment and an outdoor grill specializing in burgers, hot dogs and ribs. The indoor restaurant has the most variety, and has the added attraction of air-conditioned comfort.

Pat Dailey's Tavern at the Bay
820 Catawba Ave.
419-285-7287

Pat Dailey is somewhat of a fixture on Put-in-Bay, having long entertained folks with his island style music at the local hangouts. A few years ago he decided to give the restaurant business a try, and bought the old Cooper's Restaurant near the winery (don't be fooled — it's not on the bay, and there's no view of the water). The result is a success — witness the crowds waiting for a table at lunch time. The menu is a little more adventurous than other island eateries, with its oriental chicken salad and pasta dishes, and the perch sandwiches are quite good. There's indoor dining and an outdoor patio, also a bar and gift shop on the lower level. One of the Tavern's greatest appeals is its location away from the rowdiness of some of the downtown establishments.

Getting there:

Miller Boat Line (1-800-500-2421 or 419-285-2421) carries passengers and vehicles between Catawba and the island every half-hour during the summer, less often in the spring and fall. The ferry drops passengers off at the lime kiln dock, about a mile from downtown. Bicycle or golf cart rentals are available, or a bus will take you into town for a buck. The Jet Express (1-800-245-1538) carries passengers only from Port Clinton to downtown Put-in-Bay. Neuman Cruise and Ferry Line (1-800-876-1907) offers a two-island cruise on its luxury ship, the Emerald Empress. The boat leaves from Sandusky and stops at Put-in-Bay and Kelleys Island. Sandusky Boat Line's City of Sandusky (1-800-426-6286 or 419-627-0198) sails from Sandusky to Put-in-Bay, Middle Bass and Kelleys Island for a one-day tour of the three islands. The Goodtime I (1-800-446-3140 or 419-625-9692) runs one-day excursions to Put-in-Bay and Kelleys Island from Sandusky. Griffing Flying Service (1-800-368-3743 or 419-626-5161) has year-round service from Sandusky.

There are restrictions on bringing cars to the island at certain times. Call the individual ferry lines for information.

For more information contact the Put-in-Bay Chamber of Commerce, PO Box 250, Put-in-Bay, OH 43456 (419-285-2832) or the Sandusky/Erie County Visitors and Convention Bureau, 231 W. Washington Row, Sandusky, OH 44870; 1-800-255-ERIE.

Middle Bass Island

The castle-like facade of Lonz Winery on Middle Bass Island looks across the water directly at Put-in-Bay. Every day during the summer, ferries from the mainland and South Bass discharge hundreds of visitors who descend on the winery to enjoy the wine and live entertainment. Few venture any further. Which is probably just fine with the residents of this quiet, pretty island.

Legend has it that in 1680 the ship Griffin stopped here on its voyage, the first exploration of the lake by white men. Father Louis Hennepin, a Jesuit priest, said Mass on the island, probably the first Christian service to take place on any of the Lake Erie islands. These French explorers named the island Isle de Fleurs, Island of Flowers. It later acquired the considerably less poetic name of Middle Bass.

Middle Bass, like South Bass, was once owned by J. D. Rivera. In the late 1850s he sold most of the island to an American, George Caldwell, and to three German immigrants, Andrew Wehrle, William Rehberg and Joseph Miller. In 1863 he sold his last remaining parcel to John Lutz. Also like South Bass, the island was ideal for grape growing since the warm lake waters circulate through the island's porous limestone base, warming the earth late into the growing season.

The settlers planted grapes, and Wehrle and Miller both established wineries. Wehrle's winery, begun in 1864, was called the Golden Eagle Winery. Today, it is the site of the Lonz Winery. Although the frame building over the cellars burned in 1923, Lonz still uses the original Wehrle cellars. In 1867 Joseph Miller (or Mueller, before the name became Americanized) established a winery on his property. It was maintained by his grandson, Leslie Bretz, and was known as the Bretz Winery.

Rehberg, meanwhile, dabbled in real estate, selling off plots of land on which cottages were built. This became the Middle Bass Club, established in 1874 by some Toledo business hot-shots. It eventually evolved into an exclusive summer resort for the wealthy and influential of Toledo, Columbus, Dayton and Louisville. Four American presidents — Grover Cleveland, Benjamin Harrison, William Howard Taft and Rutherford B. Hayes stayed at the club during their terms of office. The club house was destroyed in 1949, but many of the cottages are still standing.

Ferries disembark close to the Lonz Winery (419-285-5411), where visitors can tour the cellars, sample the wines, have light snacks and enjoy live entertainment. Oddly enough, wine is no longer produced at the winery. The grapes used in Lonz wines are grown on privately-owned North Bass Island and shipped to the mainland for processing. The bottled wine is then shipped back to the winery for sale.

There are no golf cart rentals here; most people who want to explore bring bikes or rent them on the island. The quiet, paved road wanders past the center of town with its one-room school-house and 1877-vintage Town Hall that remains the center of island activity. On its way to the island's northeastern tip the road winds past a lagoon where turtles snooze in the sunshine on water lily beds.

Where to stay:

Bass Isle Resort and Camping
Middle Bass Island, OH 43446
419-285-6121, 1-800-837-5211

Though not a resort in the traditional sense, Bass Isle offers quiet, economical accommodations at the lake's edge. In addition to tent and RV sites, the resort has several cabins, the largest of which can sleep eight people. Most have kitchens and bathrooms, and some are air-conditioned. The prices are quite reasonable, making Bass Isle a nice alternative to the somewhat expensive accommodations on South Bass. The Sonny-S ferry runs every hour during the summer to Put-in-Bay, so visitors staying on Middle Bass can easily enjoy the best of both worlds.

Getting there:

Miller Boat Line (1-800-500-2421 or 419-285-2421) operates between Catawba and Middle Bass, carrying both passengers and vehicles (reservations are required). Sonny-S Ferry (419-285-8774) from Put-in-Bay carries passengers and bicycles (no bikes on weekends or holidays). Sandusky Boat Line's City of Sandusky (1-800-426-6286 or 419-627-0198) sails from Sandusky to the Put-in-Bay, Middle Bass and Kelleys Island for a one-day tour of the three islands. Griffing Flying Service (1-800-368-3743 or 419-626-5161) has year-round service from Sandusky.

For more information contact the Sandusky/Erie County Visitors and Convention Bureau, 231 W. Washington Row, Sandusky, OH 44870; 1-800-255-ERIE.

Kelleys Island

At 2,800 acres, Kelleys Island is the largest of the American Islands. It sits off to itself, three-and-a-half miles north of the Marblehead Peninsula. It is far removed, physically and in spirit, from the tourist frenzy of Put-in-Bay. Not that there isn't tourism here — ferries deposit visitors daily during the summer — but it's just more relaxed than its neighbor to the west.

Only a few squatters lived on the island in 1833 when the Kelley brothers, Datus and Irad, bought the place and changed the name from Cunningham's Island to Kelleys. The land was covered with forests of red cedar, which the Kelleys began to cut and sell for lumber, much of which was burned for the engines of the first lake steamers. The brothers divided their land into small plots and sold them to hand-picked buyers. They were a fussy pair, screening applicants and only accepting those they judged to be hard-working and thrifty.

The newcomers farmed the land and quarried limestone from the island's huge deposits. The island soon caught the attention of German immigrants who heard of its suitability for grape growing. By the turn of the century, vineyards covered the parts

The Kelley Mansion, built in the 1860s from limestone.

of the island that weren't being quarried.

It was the limestone business that really put Kelleys Island on the map. The seemingly inexhaustible supply of stone was used for building canal locks, breakwaters, and homes, some as far away as Buffalo. When the steel and iron industry fired up in Cleveland and Pittsburgh, the demand increased. A thousand acres were given over to quarrying. Immigrants from Italy, Greece, Hungary, Poland and other south and central European countries came to the island to work the stone, giving the island a decidedly European feel. When he wrote his book *Lake Erie* in 1945, historian Harlan Hatcher said of Kelleys, "*It was common a few years ago to see barefoot peasant women in native costumes with handkerchiefs or flowers on their heads gossiping together in the quarry villages.*"

It all ended in 1940, when the Kelley Island Lime & Transport Company closed the quarries and the workers left the island. At the height of the limestone business nearly 1,000 people lived on the island. The population quickly dropped to 600; now it stands

The Glacial Grooves on Kelleys Island.

at about 100 year-round residents.

Ferries let passengers off in the downtown commercial area on Lakeshore Drive, which is lined with gift shops and restaurants. This center of island business is small, though, and the commercial establishments quickly give way to ornate Victorian homes, both to the east and the west of downtown. Because much of the original architecture has been preserved, the entire island is listed as a National Historic District.

Remember those little mechanical monkeys that played bongos and guitar? Or how about Bozo the Clown? Surely you remember Howdy Doody? For a big dose of nostalgia, go see them, along with 1,000 other toys of days past, at the Lake Erie Toy Museum (419-746-2451), in Caddy Shack Square on Division Street in town. The small museum, which is a big hit with kids, houses toys from the 1800s to 1970, including such favorites as Star Wars and Sesame Street characters, Casper the Friendly Ghost, Popeye, Denis the Menace and Charlie McCarthy.

On the lake shore just east of the business district is Inscription Rock. Although its surface has been worn by centuries of weather and careless visitors, it's still possible to make out many of the engraved pictures of animals, birds and humans. A plaque shows what the carvings must have looked like originally. A roof has been built over the huge rock, which measures 32 by 21 feet. The site is now managed by the Ohio Historical Society.

The impressive mansion across the street from Inscription Rock is the Kelley Mansion, former home of Addison Kelley, son of Datus. It was built from 1861 to 1865 of local limestone and given to Addison as a wedding present. Its most distinctive feature may be the circular oak staircase that is held together without the benefit of a single nail. Local lore has it that the staircase was built in London and hauled out to the island in sections.

Today, the Kelley Mansion is an inn and a museum, open to the public for a small admission fee.

Traveling north out of town on Division Street, visitors will find a several attractions. The Kelleys Island Wine Co. (419-746-2537), located on an acre of grassy, shaded lawn off Woodford Road, has something for all members of the family. Grown-ups can sit at the outdoor tables and enjoy wine and food from the gourmet deli while the children roam and have fun in the play area provided. There are three horseshoe courts and a volleyball court, a tasting room and a gift shop. Wine selections are primarily of the somewhat sweet variety, with names like Glacial White, Sunset Pink, and Long Sweet Red. Indian Red is dry, as is the Chardonnay that is sometimes available.

Farther north on Division Street is a small museum highlighting island history located in the Old Stone Church.

Almost at the north end of Division Street is the Butterfly Box (419-746-2454), a unique gift shop and indoor butterfly garden in which North American butterflies fly freely. There is a small fee to walk through the garden, which is filled with flowering plants that provide nectar for the many butterflies.

The most popular attraction on Kelleys Island, located at the north end of Division Street, is also its oldest. Thirty thousand years ago, a glacier passed over the area, dragging boulders of granite on its underside over the soft island limestone. The glacier left grooves in the stone 2,000 feet long, 36 feet wide and 17 feet deep. Unfortunately, these Glacial Grooves were disregarded by the quarries, which mined most of the area despite its significance. Today the grooves, which are in Kelleys Island State Park (419-746-2546), are protected and maintained by the Ohio Historical Society. The 396 feet of remaining grooves are fenced in, with a walkway and interpretive signs surrounding them.

The park also has a sandy beach with changing facilities, picnic areas with grills, a campground, a boat launch ramp and more than five miles of hiking trails. The East Quarry Trail is an especially good place to view fossils embedded in the rock. There are more hiking trails through an abandoned quarry on the middle of the island. The entrance is on the south side of Ward Road.

Where to stay:

Like South Bass Island, there are so many different accommodations on Kelleys Island that this guide can't begin to cover them all. Here are a few special places.

Eagle's Nest Bed and Breakfast
216 Cameron Road
PO Box 762
Kelleys Island, OH 43438
419-746-2708 (summer)
419-625-9635 (winter)

Tucked into a wooded area away from town, the Eagle's Nest looks every bit like a turn of the century Bavarian cottage. The main building was, in fact, a quarrier's cottage, which accounts for its distinctive European appearance. It is actually more than a B & B, since each of the three rooms has a kitchenette, private bath and sundeck. One of the choices is a one-bedroom suite that includes a living room. Rooms can accommodate two, three or four people. Owners Mark and Robin Volz serve an expanded continental breakfast and make bicycles available to their guests. There are also grills and campfire rings on the property. This is

Water's Edge Retreat on Kelleys Island.

an especially good value.

Chalet East
PO Box 512
Kelleys Island, OH 43438
419-746-2335 (summer)
941-624-3811 (winter)

Chalet East, located on quiet Lakeshore Drive east of town, caters to families with children. There are two new, fully furnished apartments, each with kitchen, living room, bath, grill and deck overlooking the lake. The larger, two bedroom unit also has a dining room. Owner Emma Dalpiaz takes great pride in her place — it is spotless and meticulously maintained.

Zettlers Lakefront Bed and Breakfast
PO Box 747
Kelleys Island, OH 43438
419-746-2315

This is a traditional, adult-oriented B & B located in town across the street from the lake. The house, which was built in 1892, is bright and airy, with yellow pine floors in the guest rooms and a parlor overlooking the lake. A small private deck on the water offers a good place for fishing, swimming or sunning. A full breakfast is served each morning in the parlor. There are four bedrooms and two full baths. Owners Toby and Nora Zettler also operate the Kelleys Island Wine Co.

Water's Edge Retreat
827 East Lakeshore Drive
PO Box 839
Kelleys Island, OH 43438
419-746-2455

Looking for luxury? Look no further. This is pampering with a capital P. Water's Edge may well be the finest accommodation on the lake. A few years ago, owners Tim and Beth decided to open the perfect Victorian B & B. Not content with any of the existing buildings on the island, they set out to build one. But first they toured the entire East Coast, gathering ideas from Maine to Florida. The result is Water's Edge, a brand new, three-story, gorgeous Victorian home on a quiet street overlooking the lake. All rooms are elegantly decorated and have air-conditioning and private baths, some with Jacuzzi tubs. Wine and cheese are served each evening, and a gourmet full breakfast is prepared every morning (Beth studied cooking in Paris and Munich). An exercise room occupies the lower level. A massage therapist is available by appointment. Beth and Tim truly enjoy their guests' company and have been known to take them for a spin on their 35-foot sailboat. The price? If you have to ask, you probably can't afford it. But if you can, it's well worth it.

Where to eat:

Kenny's Place
Lakeshore Drive
419-746-2333

Kenny's Place, a new addition to the dining scene on Kelleys Island, offers a refreshing alternative to the usual island fare of burgers and dogs. Homemade soups, fresh salads, imaginative pasta dishes and well prepared steaks, chicken and seafood are the specialties here. Chef/owner Kenny came to the island with corporate restaurant experience under his belt — he knows what he's doing, and it shows. Located on the grounds of the Kelley Mansion overlooking the lake, the restaurant building was once the mess hall for a summer camp run by the Ohio Dominican Nuns. Kenny's does not have a liquor license — an unfortunate circumstance, since the food would be perfectly complemented by a nice bottle of wine.

Fresch's Island House
Division Street
419-746-2304

Housed in a Victorian home in the downtown business district, Fresch's specializes in Italian and continental cuisine. They're open for breakfast, lunch and dinner seven days a week. The restaurant is air-conditioned and has full liquor service.

Water Street Cafe
101 W. Lakeshore Drive
419-746-2468

Built in 1888 as a grocery, the building now occupied by the Water Street Cafe has seen continuous business of one sort or another since then. The owners of the restaurant have done a fine job of restoring the interior, complete with a Victorian color scheme and hammered tin ceiling. Don't expect anything fancy, but the perch sandwiches are worth a stop.

Getting there:

Both Neuman Cruise and Ferry Line (1-800-876-1907) and Kelleys Island Ferry Boat Lines (419-798-9763 or 1-800-22KIFBL) have daily ferry service from Marblehead to the island. Neuman Boat Line also offers a two-island cruise on the luxury ship, Emerald Empress. The boat leaves from Sandusky and stops at Put-in-Bay and Kelleys Island. Sandusky Boat Line's City of Sandusky (1-800-426-6286 or 419-627-0198) sails from Sandusky to Put-in-Bay, Middle Bass and Kelleys Island for a one-day tour of the three islands. The Goodtime I (1-800-446-3140 or 419-625-9692) runs one-day excursions to Put-in-Bay and Kelleys Island from Sandusky. The Island Hopper (419-734-4336 or 1-800-90-

Visitors to Pelee Island are met by the Pelee Island Winery bus.

FERRY) has daily service between Kelleys Island and Put-in-Bay. Griffing Flying Service (800-368-3743 or 419-626-5161) has year-round service from Sandusky.

For more information contact the Kelleys Island Chamber of Commerce, PO Box 783 Dept. FF, Kelleys Island, OH 43438, phone 419-746-2360; or the Sandusky/Erie County Visitors and Convention Bureau, 231 W. Washington Row, Sandusky, OH 44870; 1-800-255-ERIE.

Pelee Island

Ten-thousand-acre Pelee Island is the largest of the Lake Erie islands and the most rural. It is also the only inhabited Canadian island in the lake and the southernmost inhabited point in all of Canada. Because of this, and because the tempering effect of the lake results in the proliferation of species rare at such a latitude, Pelee Islanders recognize their home as something special.

Nature lovers have a field day on Pelee. More than 800 species of plants grow on the island, including wild hyacinth, yellow horse gentian, and delicate Miami mist. During the summer, prickly pear cactus blooms here. Swallowtail butterflies flourish, and the endangered Lake Erie water snake and the blue racer still find a home on Pelee. During the spring and summer migrations, the island is popular with bird watchers, who come to see the orioles, warblers, cuckoos and vireos that stop off on their journey across the lake. Great egrets, great blue herons and black-crowned night herons are common sights.

Much of the island is farmland, and though roads provide access to most of the shoreline and much of the interior, most of the road surface is unpaved. The town, located at the West Dock, has only a couple of eating spots, the customs house, a library, the town hall and a museum. For visitors, the attraction is primarily peace, quiet and nature. Many come to cycle the gravel roads and explore the island's nature preserves. Others come to visit the Pelee Island Winery, known for its excellent products. Spring and fall bring bird watchers to Pelee, one of the best places along the lake to spot migrating species. For few weekends each fall, the island swarms with hunters who come for the annual pheasant hunts.

Although it looks vastly different than it must have when the first white explorers came upon it, during the last hundred years the island hasn't changed nearly as much as its American counterparts. Like them, Pelee was once covered with forests and inhabited by Indians. The first white settler (who was actually half Indian) was Thomas McKee, who leased the island from the Indians for three bushels of corn a year. In 1823, William McCormick bought Pelee for $300. He brought his wife and 11 children to the island, and from that point on, the history of Pelee is peppered with the McCormick name.

Nearly half the island was marshland, infested with flies and mosquitoes. Nonetheless McCormick persuaded tenants to come live in the cabins he built. He began to clear the forests, selling the red cedar and oak for good prices. After he died, a large parcel of the land was bought by Lemuel Brown and John M. Scudder, both Americans. The appearance of the island today is largely due to the efforts of these two settlers.

Scudder had visited Holland and was impressed by the system of dikes and canals that kept the North Sea at Bay. He envisioned the same for Pelee Island and slowly, he accomplished it. Four thousand acres were drained and crops were planted on what had previously been a swamp. The land is still drained today by the same method, an arrangement that also works to irrigate the land during summer dry spells.

Vineyards flourished, and later, tobacco. Soybeans and corn appeared. Agriculture became, and has remained, the island's mainstay.

Most visitors arrive on Pelee at the West Dock via the ferries that run from both the U.S. and Canadian sides. While it's possible to drive around the perimeter of the island, the road is paved only on the western side. East-West Road, which runs across the south end, is also paved. Most "attractions" are on West Shore Road and at the two ends of the island. Unpaved East Shore Road is occupied mainly with private cottages, as this is the sandy side of the island. There are also a couple of public beaches. The water is very shallow here, and usually quite calm and clear, making these beaches ideal for children.

Just south of the West Dock is the Heritage Centre Museum (519-724-2291). This small collection should be the first stop for anyone coming to the island. With displays of both the natural and human history of the island, it offers a good perspective of this unique place. There are artifacts from the native inhabitants, including pottery shards, tools and arrowheads, and items from more recent years, such as newspaper articles about the many settlers who attempted to cross over the ice to and from the mainland during the winter months. (Many of them failed.) Visitors will learn about the development of agriculture and viticulture on Pelee, and about the hardy souls who made both possible. The geological origins of the island and its native plants and animal species are also explored. Curator Ron Thiessen is part philosopher, part biologist, part historian, and a full-scale walking encyclopedia on Pelee. He has written several short books about the island which interested visitors will find invalu-

The abandoned lighthouse at Lighthouse Point Provincial Nature Reserve on Pelee Island.

able. They are for sale at the museum.

The Pelee Island Wine Pavilion (519-724-2469) is south of the West Dock on East-West Rd. While the winery's grapes are grown on the island, production is done in Kingsville, Ontario. These are some of the best wines found along Lake Erie. They include Chardonnay, Pinot Noir, Pinot Gris, Gewurztraminer and many other varietals. At the pavilion there's a retail store and large outdoor dining area with a large open-air barbecue. Visitors can cook their own burgers, chicken or sausage on the grill and relax with a bottle of wine. The winery offers tram tours to its vineyards in the island's interior with a tasting among the vines. There are also wine appreciation seminars several times daily.

Going farther south beyond the winery the shore road becomes gravel and its name changes to McCormick Rd. It ends at the entrance to Fish Point Provincial Nature Reserve, where there is a small parking lot. A trail leads through the woods, past Fox

Pond and out to a sand spit that juts into the lake for some distance. The trail offers opportunities to spot migrating birds in the spring and fall, and a variety of animals, birds and plants the rest of the year. Painted turtles and bullfrogs are common at Fox Pond, as are Great Blue Herons and wood ducks. Visitors are cautioned to stay on the trail, both because of the rare species that may be damaged from trampling and because of the abundance of poison ivy. After the second week or so of May this is the domain of the mosquitoes — wear long sleeves, long pants and use insect repellent. Wading into the lake off the sand spit is dangerous, as currents are often strong and the sand is subject to shifts.

Just off the northwest corner of the island is a limestone rock jutting from the water known as Hulda's Rock. The legend surrounding this rock has been passed from generation to generation, and though there's no telling how much there is to it, the bittersweet tale lives on. Hulda was a young woman, the daughter of an Indian chief and a French woman from Montreal who had been captured and brought to the island. Hulda fell in love with an Englishman who came to the island with other explorers. He stayed behind and they married. Their happy life together was disrupted when he learned that his mother was dying. Before he left to see her on her deathbed, he promised Hulda he would return. What came instead was a letter telling Hulda that he had found someone else. In despair she leapt to her death from the rock that bears her name.

At the very north point of the island, accessible from Eastshore Road, is Lighthouse Point Provincial Nature Reserve. The trail that begins at the road runs past Lake Henry, a marsh that was created in the 1970s when a dike holding out lake water broke, flooding the area. It's now home to herons, egrets, cormorants, ducks and geese, as well as the occasional raptor or two. On the opposite side of the trail is a canal heavily populated by painted turtles and bullfrogs, along with some snapping turtles. The trail ends at the beach, from which it's a short walk north to an abandoned lighthouse built in 1833 of island limestone. The rocks around the base of the lighthouse are a favorite sunning spot for Lake Erie water snakes, an endangered species found only in the western basin of Lake Erie.

Over the Lake Tours offers 45-minute guided tours of the highlights on Pelee Island departing from the West Dock at 11:00 a.m., noon, 1:30 p.m. and 2:30 p.m., weekends only.

Where to stay:

Pelee has no resorts or large tourist complexes, which is part of its charm. There are, however, many types of accommodations. Though this listing includes only inns and B & Bs, cottages may better suit the needs of some. Cottage rental information can be obtained by writing the Public Relations office at the address at the end of this section.

Stonehill Bed & Breakfast
West Shore Road
Pelee Island, Ontario N0R 1M0
519-724-2193

Becky and Hayward Strowbridge's 1875 stone home has a beautiful location overlooking the lake north of the West Dock. There are four rooms, decorated in country style, and one shared bath. Full breakfast is provided and bicycle rentals are available. There's a private beach close by. But probably the Stonehill's nicest feature is the large, shaded verandah that faces an expanse of green lawn and tall trees framed by the blue of the lake beyond. Children over 13 are welcome. Stonehill is open year-round.

The Tin Goose Inn
1060 East-West Road
Pelee Island, Ontario N0R 1M0
519-724-2223

There's nothing else quite like the Tin Goose Inn on Pelee. Located in a century-old restored Victorian building at the isolated east side of the island, the inn is the picture-perfect romantic getaway. Run by Trevor Loop and his sister, Tara, the inn features eight guest rooms and four shared baths. Each room is decorated in an elegant country-Victorian style, with themes such as the "Vineyard Room," the "Music Room" and the "Ruby Room." The staff is professional and attentive, and the on-site restaurant, Gooseberry's Island Cuisine, is excellent. Guests are

Visitor with his horse on Pelee Island.

served complimentary wine and hors d'oeuvres every afternoon in the sitting room or on the outdoor patio reserved exclusively for them. There is a small beach just opposite the inn. Kayak and bicycle rentals are available.

Anchor and Wheel Inn
11 West Shore Rd.
Pelee Island, Ontario N0R 1M0
519-724-2195

There's something for everyone at the Anchor and Wheel, one of the oldest lodging establishments on the island. The main building houses a B & B and the Island Restaurant. Across the parking lot is a small motel, while just down the street there is an area for family trailer camping. A large grassy field serves for tent camping. The B & B has six bright, cheery rooms and two large, clean baths. The motel has rooms with private baths, including some with Jacuzzis. A large "Bunkroom" has five sets of bunk beds and an adjoining bath. Children are welcome at both the B & B and motel. Prices are quite reasonable, and the place is kept very clean by the friendly staff, making this a good choice for those looking for something simple and economical. The restaurant serves tasty food in a casual atmosphere.

The Gathering Place
West Shore Road
Pelee Island, Ontario N0R 1M0
519-724-2656

This old stone house was built in 1893 using island limestone. It is right next door to the Stonehill B & B and shares its lovely view of the water. Owners Sandy McDonald and Maeve Omstead describe the sunsets as "better than Key West." There are three guest rooms, one with private bath, the others with a shared bath. A library with fireplace and a screened in front porch add to the relaxed country ambiance. Bike rentals are available for guests. Open May through November.

Where to eat:

Gooseberry's Island Cuisine (at the Tin Goose Inn)
1060 East-West Road
519-724-2223

Gooseberry's, located in the Tin Goose Inn on the east side of the island, is a cheery, intimate restaurant in a restored Victorian house. The food is elegant, the service good, and the atmosphere cozy. This is the perfect island place for a romantic dinner. If you are staying at one of the island's B & Bs, the staff at Gooseberry's will be happy to shuttle you to the restaurant for a small fee.

The Island Restaurant (at Anchor & Wheel Inn)
11 West Shore Rd.
519-724-2195

Walk into the Island Restaurant on a Saturday night and the place is filled with islanders, a sure sign that there's something good in store. For many, that something is the best walleye likely to be found anywhere on the lake — sweet, fresh-as-can-be, lightly breaded and pan fried with white wine, shallots, mushrooms and almonds. It's a casual place decorated in a nautical theme. Bird lovers will enjoy watching the orioles and hummingbirds that are attracted by feeders that manager Barb hangs in the surrounding trees to attract avian visitors.

Getting there:

Ferries run daily from spring through fall from both the Canadian and American sides. From the States you can catch the ferry at Sandusky. From Canada, the ferries run from Leamington or Kingsville, depending on the time of year. Passengers who wish to transport cars must have reservations. For more information, contact Pelee Island Transportation at 1-800-661-2220 or 519-724-2115. Griffing Flying Service (800-368-3743 or 419-626-5161) has year-round service from Sandusky. For more information contact Public Relations, Pelee Island, Ontario, Canada N0R 1M0.

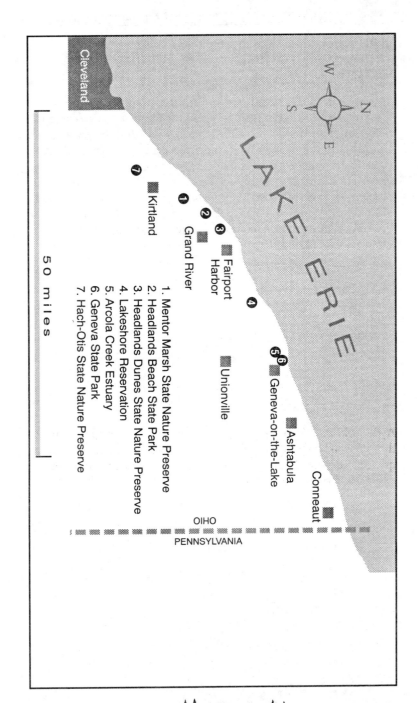

LAKE ERIE

Cleveland

N
W E
S

50 miles

7 Kirtland

1 Grand River

2
3 Fairport
Harbor

4 Unionville

5 6 Geneva-on-the-Lake

Ashtabula

Conneaut

OIHO
PENNSYLVANIA

1. Mentor Marsh State Nature Preserve
2. Headlands Beach State Park
3. Headlands Dunes State Nature Preserve
4. Lakeshore Reservation
5. Arcola Creek Estuary
6. Geneva State Park
7. Hach-Otis State Nature Preserve

Chapter *Three*

Ohio's Eastern Shore
Vineyards and Covered Bridges

Just beyond Cleveland's sprawl, northeast Ohio settles into an area of small towns and countryside quite unlike the western shoreline. Ohio's eastern shore saw the same rapid development in the 1800s and the same decline after Cleveland pulled far out in the lead during the 19th century. But unlike the towns of Ohio's western shore, the east — with the exception of the resort town, Geneva-on-the-Lake — continue to this day to rely on industry, not tourism, to earn a living.

Ashtabula and Conneaut are still busy ports, though not what they were in their heyday. Once-bustling Fairport Harbor is now quiet. And Grand River, at one time a center of the commercial fishing industry, regressed to a sleepy town when pollution levels impacted the fish population.

Slowly, though, the towns are awakening to the potential of tourism. Ashtabula has its restored historical district, Bridge Street. Conneaut promotes its covered bridges. Geneva-on-the-Lake, which has always been a party town, is making a comeback as a place for wholesome entertainment after a few years of unsavory reputation. Wineries line the edge of the lake, attracting visitors from all over Ohio who come to sample the surprisingly good wares.

There's plenty to be discovered in this part of Ohio. You just

have to slow down and look a little harder.

PLACES
Fairport Harbor/Grand River

These two small towns sit on either side of the Grand River. Walk down a quiet street in Fairport Harbor and you'll find it hard to believe that in 1845 there were four hotels in town. A couple of honky-tonk bars completed the picture for this busy port of the mid-1800s where $1,000,000 worth of commerce passed through the harbor in 1847 alone.

During the Civil War, Fairport Harbor was a hot-bed of anti-slavery activities. It wasn't unusual for slaves to be hidden in the cellars of the hotels that housed slave-hunters from the South only a few floors above.

After the war, new pier facilities and an extension of the railroad to Pittsburgh brought a new influx of settlers. Finns, Slovaks and Hungarians flocked to the town to work on the docks. Shocked by the saloons and loose living of the town, they built churches and formed a temperance society that had a profound effect on the town's character from that point on.

Today, the only thing that's likely to draw visitors is the Fairport Marine Museum (440-354-4825), housed partially in the brick lighthouse built at the mouth of the Grand River in 1823. Founded in 1945, the museum was the first lighthouse marine museum in the United States. Exhibits include navigational charts and instruments, nautical paintings, models, lanterns and other items of historical interest. There are also artifacts from the early Indian inhabitants of the area who had established a major village that was discovered by archaeologists in the 1930s. The museum is open seasonally, from Memorial Day through Labor Day.

While Fairport found its fortune — for a time — in port commerce, Grand River found its living in the fishing industry. Although records prior to 1900 have not survived, historians know that by 1910, commercial fisheries were bringing in one to two million pounds of fish a year. Fish processing plants lined the Grand River a mile inland. Pike, sturgeon, yellow perch and walleye were shipped by rail to New York, Scranton, Buffalo, Chicago and St. Louis. But by 1961 the annual catch had declined to 32,000 pounds. By 1968, the commercial fishing industry at Grand River was dead, and even the retail fish stores in town brought their goods in from Vermilion.

The only remnants of tiny Grand River's past as a center of commercial fishing exist in the form of two notable seafood restaurants. Brennan's Fish House (440-354-9785) serves up some of the best perch and walleye dinners around, overflowing with great home-made fries. Pickle Bill's (440-352-6343), right next door, has an extensive seafood menu served in an eclectic atmosphere. It's almost as much fun to look at the place as it is to eat there. Both are on River Street.

Geneva-on-the-Lake

Back in the days before theme parks, families went to places like Geneva-on-the-Lake to have fun. Not many small resort towns survived the arrival of the Six Flags of the world, but somehow Geneva-on-the-Lake did. If you have kids, take them. They'll love it. There's a mile-long strip with video games, go-carts, a shooting gallery, putt-putt golf and enough junk food to keep you greased up for a year. Hot dogs, doughnuts, fries, pizza, and barbecued chicken beckon from the sidewalks. The lake shines blue just beyond the strip, and the sounds of revelry are in the air.

The town comes by its reputation for fun honestly. Unlike the hard-working ports of Ashtabula and Conneaut, Geneva-on-the-Lake has been a holiday town from the beginning. In 1869, a picnic area was opened at Sturgeon Point (now occupied by condos), and shortly after, a dance hall was built. When visitors began coming and setting up tents, cottages and boarding houses sprang up.

By the early 1900s the town was attracting the likes of Henry

Driving go-carts at Geneva-on-the-Lake.

Ford, John D. Rockefeller, and Harvey Firestone who, ironically, chose to camp instead of patronizing the fancy boarding houses they well could have afforded. Until the automobile put Geneva-on-the-Lake within just about everyone's reach, the town was known as a resort for bluebloods only.

Then, with the advent of cars, the working class arrived. So did the Big Bands. Tommy Dorsey, Glenn Miller, Duke Ellington, Cab Calloway, Lawrence Welk — the list goes on and on. Kay Kyser was even marooned there for a summer, left high, dry and broke by his rebellious band who moved on without him.

One of the old boarding houses, the Grandview, is now a museum. The Jennie Munger Gregory Museum (440-466-7337), named for its last owner, sits far back from the road overlooking the lake west of the Strip. The house was built in 1823 by the first landowner of the township, Thomas Fitch, at the site named Fitch's Landing in his honor. The wooden structure originally served as a farmhouse, but in later years joined the ranks of the boarding houses. Jennie Munger Gregory donated the house to

Enjoying the water slide at Geneva-on-the-Lake.

the Ashtabula County Historical Society to use as a base for its operations.

The museum is decorated with period furnishings, including some of Mrs. Gregory's belongings. There is a large Victorian sitting room and several bedrooms named for previous owners. Mrs. Fitch's room is decorated in the style of the 1830s, when the house was built. Mrs. Putman's room reflects the world of the 1860s. A nice collection of 1920s beaded purses is featured in Mrs. Gregory's room, which also contains her marble-topped dresser and wash stand.

The museum is open during the summer, or by appointment at other times of the year. A Victorian Christmas is celebrated on the first two Sundays in December each year.

Another building of note is the old one-room schoolhouse, which stands in Township Park just east of the Strip. The brick structure was built in 1883 on the foundation of an earlier wooden building erected in 1838. It was used as a school until 1909, when the local children were sent to a newer, nearby three-room schoolhouse.

In keeping with its tradition, Geneva-on-the-Lake has its own amusement park. Erieview Park (440-466-8650) has been in the business of making folks smile for more than 50 years now. There are rides — some suitable for very small children—two huge waterslides, a concession stand, a picnic area overlooking the lake, and a large arcade. If you're not one for rides, plop yourself down at a picnic table with a good book and let the kids have a ball —the place is small enough that they can't get lost, but big enough to offer plenty to do.

CYCLING TIPS

From Grand River east to the Ashtabula County line, near Geneva-on-the-Lake, it's impossible to ride along the lake for any distance, since there is no continuous road within sight of the water. Once you get to the county line, however, it's a different story. Route 534 winds through Geneva-on-the-Lake and on for about nine miles to Ashtabula, right by the water's edge. There's little traffic, and the scenery is pleasant. Riding through Ashtabula can be a bit difficult, with congestion and some traffic lights, but once beyond, it's smooth sailing all the way to Conneaut, about 12 miles away. Inland, Ashtabula County is rural and beautiful, especially in fall when the foliage is turning. If you're tempted to explore the backroads, though, haul out your mountain or hybrid bike — Ashtabula County has more unpaved roads than any other county in Ohio.

The Old Firehouse Winery, just west of Erieview, also has a large picnic area. They serve food and their own wines (which are surprisingly good). During the summer months they offer live music in the evenings, making it a perfect place to relax after a busy day wandering the strip or swimming in the lake at nearby Geneva State Park. The winery celebrates several special events, including a polka festival (June), a Celtic Feis (August), fall clambake and a Christmas open house.

Although the town draws many day visitors from nearby areas, people still come to Geneva-on-the-Lake to spend their vacations. There are plenty of cottages and motels, and a couple of bed and breakfasts. Accommodations range from the luxurious to the down-at-the-heel, with most falling somewhere in the middle.

Except for a few holiday celebrations, once the cold weather hits, Geneva-on-the-Lake slams shut like a turtle in its shell. There's barely a sign of life on the bleak sidewalks lined with boarded-up shops. But come back in May. Just like the landscape, the town comes to life and the fun is ready to begin again.

Where to stay:

Charlma Bed and Breakfast
6739 Lake Road West
Geneva-on-the-Lake, OH 44041
440-466-3646

In 1988, owners Bob and Charlene Schaeffer began renovation on their 1918 home. The result was Charlma (named for Charlene's parents, Charles and Alma), a luxurious retreat on the Lake Erie shore. There are two rooms furnished with antiques, each with private bath. A spacious porch, complete with Jacuzzi, overlooks the lake. The house is in a quiet residential area just west of Geneva State Park. While the action in town is not within walking distance, it's an easy five-minute drive. The Schaeffers provide a bottle of local wine and a full home-made breakfast. Smoking and pets are not allowed. Charlma is open seasonally, so be sure to call before planning a visit.

Where to eat:

Old Firehouse Winery
Geneva-on-the-Lake, OH
440-466-9300

There's nothing fancy about the food here — it's one step above the carnival-type fare that permeates the town. But you'll get some good wings and even a decent dish of pasta if you don't mind paper plates. The wines are good and the view of the lake is perfect. During the summer they're open every day, but things

The Old Firehouse Winery in Geneva-on-the-Lake.

taper off in the winter, when they're likely to be open just on weekends.

Mary's Kitchen
5023 New Street
440-466-8606

Just off the main drag, Mary's Kitchen offers a healthy alternative to hot dogs and fries. Home-cooked meals, not a culinary adventure, await the diner at Mary's. Open seven days a week for three meals a day, this is a dependable place for fueling up.

For more information contact Geneva-on-the-Lake Visitor's Bureau, 5336 Lake Rd., Geneva-on-the-Lake, OH 44041; 1-800-862-9948; or Ashtabula County Convention and Visitor's Bureau, 36 W. Walnut St., Jefferson, OH 44047; 440-576-4707 or 1-800-3-DROP IN.

Ashtabula

A hundred years ago, Ashtabula was a rowdy, hard-drinking, hard-living harbor town that played host to thousands of sailors. Today, it's still a working port, shipping the coal that arrives by rail from the mines of West Virginia and southern Ohio across the lake to Canada and west to the steel mills of Cleveland and Lorain.But today's auto-mated unloading means smaller crews and faster turnaround. Sailors no longer roam the streets or crowd the saloons. Instead, Bridge St., where much of the action used to take place, has been restored and is now home to antiques stores, gift shops, restau-

TOURING ASHTABULA COUNTY'S COVERED BRIDGES

With 15, Ashtabula County has the most covered bridges of all Ohio counties. While three are close to Conneaut, the rest are scattered throughout the county. Ashtabula County's Covered Bridge Committee has designed two self-guided bridge tours and a fall foliage tour. Tour A covers the northeastern part of the county and includes nine covered bridges along a 69-mile drive. An extension is added to the route to make the fall foliage tour. Tour B is in the western and southern part of the county, winding past five covered bridges in 66 miles. There are signs along the route that indicate where the bridges can be found. For a free tour map contact the Covered Bridge Committee at 25 West Jefferson Street, Jefferson, OH 44047; 440-576-3769.

rants and cafes. Many of these businesses reflect the ethnic heritage of the town that attracted immigrants from Ireland, Scotland, Italy, Finland and Sweden to work in the shipyards and on the railroads during the 19th century.

On December 29, 1876, Ashtabula became the site of what was then the largest train disaster in history. On that cold, stormy evening some 160 people plunged 75 feet into icy water when the Howe-Truss bridge over the Ashtabula river collapsed, taking the Pacific Express No. 5 with it. The train, owned by the Lake Shore and Michigan Southern Railroad was on a run from Erie, Pennsylvania, at the time. Upon impact it immediately caught fire since it was constructed largely of wood and lit by oil lamps and heated by wood-burning stoves. Most of those who survived the fall burned to death.

The final death toll was 92; 64 were injured. Many of the bodies were burned or dismembered beyond identification. They were buried in two mass graves in Ashtabula's Chestnut Grove Cemetery, where today an obelisk stands.

It was later discovered that the bridge, built and owned by the Lake Shore and Michigan Southern Railroad, was structurally unsound. Although the president of the Lake Shore and Michigan Southern Railroad, Amasa Stone, denied any defects in the bridge, Chief Engineer Charles Collins committed suicide just hours after he testified at an investigative hearing.

Today, in addition to restored Bridge Street, there is much evidence of Ashtabula's rich history. Just east of Bridge Street, the Bascule Lift Bridge spans the Ashtabula River. Built in 1925 and restored in 1986, the lift bridge replaced earlier pontoon and swing bridges. (The term "bascule" comes from the Middle ages, and refers to the type of bridge commonly used then, better known as a drawbridge.) It lifts every half-hour to allow boats to pass from the harbor into the lake.

North of Bridge Street, high on a bluff overlooking the water, is Walnut Boulevard. Lined with stately Victorian homes, it is one of the prettiest residential streets in Ashtabula. But it is also the location of two unique museums, the Great Lakes Marine & U.S. Coast Guard Memorial Museum and the Hubbard House Museum.

The Great Lakes Marine Museum (440-964-6847) opened its doors in 1984, in a house built in 1898, previously the residence of the Ashtabula lighthouse keepers and the Coast Guard Chief. The museum is filled with artifacts of life on the Great Lakes and photographs of ships in Ashtabula Harbor. The French-made Fresnel lens that was installed in the Ashtabula lighthouse in

1915 is on display here, along with models of Coast Guard boats, cargo ships, railroad carferries and passenger ships.

Lake Erie has claimed more ships per square mile than any other body of fresh water in the world, and Ashtabula has seen its share. Several wrecks still lie in the harbor; a mill stone brought from one of them is on display on the grounds of the museum. The museum also contains the only working model of a Hulett iron ore unloader. Invented by Conneaut native George Hulett in the late 1800s, the automatic unloaders revolutionized the steel industry. They allowed larger ships to be unloaded more quickly, using fewer men. "Huletts," as they were called, were installed in harbors across Lake Erie, including Conneaut, Ashtabula, Cleveland, Lorain, Huron, Sandusky and Toledo. These massive machines, capable of lifting 20-ton bites, drove ore delivery costs down dramatically, from three dollars a ton to five cents. But progress marched on, and after World War II self-unloading ships appeared. The Huletts couldn't compete with their efficiency and were gradually discontinued from use. The last four of the original eight units from Ashtabula Harbor were dismantled in 1986. A small part of one is on display in the park opposite the museum.

At the rear of the museum, overlooking the harbor, rests the pilot house from the steamer Thomas Walters. Built in 1911, in Lorain, Ohio, the ship sailed the lakes for 75 years until it was cut up for scrap in 1986. The pilot house is equipped with a working radar unit donated by the Ashtabula Campus of Kent State University. This is an excellent place to view the huge Conrail conveyor that transports coal across the river from the terminus of the rail line on the east side to the coal piles on the west side. The conveyor is capable of delivering 6,000 tons of coal an hour.

The Hubbard House Museum (440-964-8168), just down the street, was once a station for the underground railroad. Built by abolitionists William and Catharine Hubbard in the early 1840s, the house code named "Mother Hubbard's Cupboard" served as a safe place for slaves escaping across the lake to Canada. The house has been restored to its original condition and furnished with period objects from the surrounding area. The basement

One of Conneaut's three covered bridges.

houses a collection of Civil War memorabilia gathered by Ashtabula resident Charles Moses.

Just west of town Walnut Beach, an attractive, sandy beach with changing facilities and a concession stand, attracts many during the summer months.

Lake Shore Park, across the lift bridge and east of town also has a sandy beach, a playground and large picnic pavilion. This area was once the site of the Woodland Beach Park, an amusement park that drew visitors via special rail excursions from Pittsburgh, Buffalo and Youngstown. Overnight vacationers often stayed at nearby Lake Shore Park Hotel. The park thrived for a time, but fell victim to the rising popularity of cars and the greater freedom for travel they provided. It closed in 1929. The Lake Shore Park Hotel likewise closed its doors, although you can still see some of the hotel's floor boards that now serve as the floor of Hulbert's Restaurant on Bridge Street.

The octagonal house on Mill Road in Conneaut.

Where to stay:

Michael Cahill Bed & Breakfast
P.O. Box 3024
1106 Walnut Blvd.
Ashtabula, OH 44044
440-964-8449

In 1887, Irish immigrant Michael Cahill built his home on Walnut Boulevard. Over the years it fell into disrepair. By the time current owners Pat and Paul Goode bought the property it was nearly in ruins, but that didn't stop them from painstakingly restoring it to its original charm. The cherry woodwork has been refinished, the floors sanded. The house is furnished with antiques, including a couple of clawfoot bathtubs. There are four guest rooms, each with private bath, several sitting rooms, a full kitchen on the ground floor and one smaller one on the second floor, and a front porch to take in the lake breezes. The inn is open all year. The street is quiet and within easy walking distance of the historic harbor area, museums and Walnut Beach.

Where to eat:

Hulbert's Restaurant
1033 Bridge Street
440-964-2594

Located in the historic harbor area, Hulbert's was once the site of a shoe store and a drug store. Owners Betty and Jim Hulbert gutted the building and restored it to make a charming Victorian setting for indulging in home-cooked meals. The interior includes antiques from the area, including the floor from the old Lake Shore Park Hotel, wrought iron from Erie, Pennsylvania, and beautiful oval oak doors from a local house, now torn down. For more information contact the Ashtabula Area Chamber of Commerce at PO Box 6, Ashtabula, OH 44005; 216-998-6998; or Ashtabula County Convention and Visitor's Bureau, 36 W. Walnut St., Jefferson, OH 44047; 216-576-4707 or 1-800-3-DROP IN.

Conneaut

Today, visitors come to Conneaut for its covered bridges, wineries and fishing. But the first visitors came for very different reasons.

In 1796, Moses Cleaveland set out to survey land purchased by the Connecticut Land Company that would later become known as the Western Reserve. He first landed, not at his namesake, Cleveland, but at Conneaut, the easternmost Ohio town on Lake Erie. He and his party of fifty-some men and a handful of women and children christened their landing spot Fort Independence. They built a crude building to house their supplies and began the task of surveying. After the territory was staked out, they moved on west to the mouth of the Cuyahoga to continue their work.

It wasn't until 1798 that anyone settled in the area. Two families, the Montgomerys and the Wrights, stumbled upon the shelter built by Cleaveland's men and decided to set up housekeeping. They became the first permanent residents of what is now

Conneaut, a Seneca Indian word that means *"a place where snow stays late in the spring."*

By the 1820s the ship building industry was in full-swing. Sawmills, a grist mill, a distillery and a couple of foundries sprang up. Real estate boomed when rumors of a rail line spread. Only 40 years after Cleaveland had set foot next to the Conneaut Creek, the harbor was a bustling place. In 1836 it was visited by 275 sailing vessels and 760 steamers. More than a million feet of sawed lumber, 24,000 bushels of grain, over 10,000 barrels of pork and beef, and tons of coal, cheese and butter were shipped from the port.

Like all ports on the Great Lakes, some ships left Conneaut and never returned. A few, like the Marquette and Bessemer No. 2, are a mystery to this day. On December 7, 1909, the carferry left Conneaut harbor, headed for Port Stanley, Ontario. It was loaded with 32 railroad cars — not full capacity. However, Captain Robert Rowan McLeod had expressed concern about the safety of the ship saying, *"If we were caught in a heavy sea and the cars shifted, a man would not have time to put on his hat before she would be at the bottom. She would go down like a shot."*

No one knows what happened that December day. The ship was never seen again. Presumably it lies at the bottom of the lake, somewhere between Conneaut and the Canadian shore. Bodies were found, some of them frozen solid in the ice, on both the Canadian and American shores. Capt. McLeod's body washed up at Long Point, Canada. His brother, First Mate John McLeod, was found frozen in the intake at the Niagara Falls Power Company. As a result of the tragedy, safety precautions, such as installation of additional marine lighting and provisions for additional rescue crews, were instigated.

Into the 20th century, agriculture boomed and industry thrived. The rail lines were extended to the docks, allowing iron ore to be shipped. Soon after, the Hulett unloaders, invented by local George Hulett, made unloading the ore faster and cheaper. The town grew, both in population and area, and for a time things were good. The Depression hit Conneaut hard, though, and today parts of the town look as if they never recovered.

Conneaut doesn't have the holiday air of Geneva-on-the-Lake or the historical draw of Ashtabula's Bridge Street. Except for a few restaurants, the waterfront appears somewhat bleak, although nearby Township Park has one of the nicest beaches in Ohio. Downtown Conneaut, a few miles inland, still has some beautiful architecture. Take away the modern cars and signs, and it looks like old-fashioned, small-town America.

One of the more curious architectural finds are the town's two octagonal houses and one octagonal barn. One house, just off the main drag at 301 Liberty Street, is listed on the National Historic Register. The other house, an attractive red brick structure, is a bit out of town at 456 Mill Road. The barn is south of town on Hatches Corner Road. The octagonal shape is thought to have signified a stop on the Underground Railroad, which was very active in this part of the state.

The Conneaut Community Center, on Buffalo Street is the town's cultural center. Built in 1898 as a Finnish Meeting Hall for immigrants from Finland, Kilpi Hall, as it was known, served as an athletic club, a theater and a Temperance Hall. Now the building houses the community center, which offers classes in the arts and displays works of local artists and photographers. In the summer, the outside pavilion draws many who come to hear the free concerts.

Conneaut Railroad Historical Museum (440-599-7878), in the old New York Central depot on Depot Street, preserves the past of this once-teeming train stop. Trains still whiz by the depot, built in 1900, but now they carry freight, not passengers. In addition to artifacts and an extensive miniature train display, the museum is retirement home for a locomotive, car and caboose. Visitors can walk through the caboose and can see into the cab of the locomotive. The museum is open daily, Memorial Day through Labor Day.

Although the railroad museum is a draw, most people don't really come to Conneaut to see the town itself. Most come for the farther-flung attractions — the wineries and covered bridges. Because the town is so spread out (the visitors' bureau says Conneaut occupies more square miles than any city in Ohio), this section of the guide ventures farther from the Lake Erie shores than usual.

The Annual Ashtabula Covered Bridge Festival, which takes place the second weekend of October, brings many visitors to the area. Ashtabula County has more covered bridges —15 of them — than any other county in Ohio. Although nearly 60 have been built over the years, many fell into disrepair, were washed away by floods, or were destroyed by arson. Fortunately, Ashtabula County has been blessed with a county engineer who takes particular interest in covered bridges. John Smolen Jr., who has become known across the country as an expert in the field, was instrumental in the preservation of the bridges and the building of two new ones.

Many people think that covered bridges were built for their attractiveness in an era when things were built, not just with practicalities in mind, but with an eye for aesthetics. But the bridges were covered to protect the wooden road surface from the elements, thus prolonging the life-span of the bridge.

There are three covered bridges in the rural area just outside the town of Conneaut. The newest, and perhaps most picturesque, is the State Road Bridge, opened in 1983. Its latticed design makes a graceful presence spanning Conneaut Creek. Just a bit north is the Creek Road Bridge, also crossing Conneaut Creek as it meanders northward to Lake Erie. Records do not indicate when the bridge was constructed, but it was restored in 1982. The Middle Road Bridge, one of the oldest in the county, was built in 1868. It too spans the Conneaut Creek, but farther to the east. It has undergone restoration in recent years, including the addition of two support piers.

Two local wineries offer notable wines. Markko Vineyards, 4500 South Ridge Road (440-593-3197), was one of the first wineries in Northeast Ohio. Since 1968, owners Arnie Esterer and Tom Hubbard have been growing Chardonnay, Johannesburg Riesling and Cabernet Sauvignon grapes for their wines, which have won consistent acclaim for their high quality. The cozy tasting room, located down a long wooded drive from the road, is open six days a week year-round (closed on Sundays).

Stop off at Buccia Vineyard, 518 Gore Road (440-593-5976), and you'll feel like you just joined a party. Owners Fred and Joanna Bucci left the city rat race behind some 20 years ago to follow their dream, and they never looked back. Their friendliness is infectious, and it's obvious they enjoy what they do. Although most of their wine is made from hybrid grapes such as Seyval and Baco, this is the only place in the world where you can taste wine made from Agawan grapes. Don't know what that is? Ask Fred — he'll love to tell you. They also have a quite comfortable B & B on the premises.

Where to stay:

Buccia Vineyard Bed and Breakfast
518 Gore Road
Conneaut, OH 44030
440-593-5976

The Buccis have one of the best-kept secrets around. Their B & B, located at the family winery, sits back on a country road outside Conneaut. Look out the window of one of the rooms, and you'll see vineyards and woods. Each of the three rooms (soon to be four) has its own hot tub, private bath, small eating area with microwave and refrigerator, TV, CD player, and private arbor-covered deck. All for a very reasonable price. And with the winery on-premises, refreshment is never far away.

Campbell Braemar Bed and Breakfast
390 State Street
Conneaut, OH 44030
440-599-7362

Owner Mary Campbell has the B & B business in her blood. She talked about opening one with her husband, Andy, for years. He wasn't so sure. She quietly collected furniture and stored it in her basement, confident that one day her dream would come true. Then a nearby house went up for auction. She went. She bid. She got the house. But she didn't tell Andy. Two weeks went by before she had the courage to do it. After months of renovation the B & B opened. Now Andy is just as involved as Mary. A former cook in the British Army, Andy serves his homemade sausage for breakfasts and makes regular jaunts to Nova Scotia

Headlands Beach State Park.

to pick up kippers for guests. The house, which is located in the heart of Conneaut, is decorated with Scottish motifs, particularly appropriate since both Mary and Andy are natives of Scotland. It has four bedrooms, a kitchen, dining room, living room and a bath. Mary and Andy live across the street. Children are welcome, but pets are not.

Lakeland Colonial Bed & Breakfast
1145 Lake Road
Conneaut, OH 44030
440-599-8139

This is the only B & B right on the lake in the Conneaut area. Just west of town, in a quiet residential area, this house dating from 1854 has been completely renovated by owner Jeff Galiffo. There are three bedrooms with bath and a family room decorated with Civil War artifacts.

For more information contact the Conneaut Area Tourism Board, PO Box 722, Conneaut, OH 44030; phone 440-593-2402 .

NATURAL ATTRACTIONS

Mentor Marsh State Nature Preserve

Look out over Mentor Marsh and you will see a sea of waving reed grass where a river once flowed. Thousands of years ago, the Grand River made its way toward Lake Erie through the area that is now covered by the marsh. Over the years, the forces of erosion changed the course of the river, which now flows considerably farther east, leaving the wetlands that remain today.

Among the earliest proponents for preservation of the marsh was Charles M. Shipman, a member of the Burroughs Nature Club which was active in the first half of the 20th century. Today the fishing pond at the far eastern tip of the preserve bears his name. While the marsh is now protected by its preserve status, it came perilously close to destruction in the 1960s when a proposed development plan called for the area to be dredged to make way for inland waterways and docking facilities. Fortunately, this plan gave rise to a grassroots effort to save the marsh, spearheaded by the Burroughs Nature Club and its president, Harold J. Zimmerman.

Others joined in the battle to save the marsh. The Nature Conservancy, Cleveland Museum of Natural History, Cleveland Metropolitan Parks Board, Holden Arboretum, Lake County Federation of Garden Clubs, and the Cleveland and Blackbrook Audubon Societies all played a part. The Morton Salt Company, which still carries on mining operations nearby, donated surface rights to 320 acres of the marsh to the state; while the Diamond Alkali Company granted surface rights to 90 acres to the Nature Conservancy. The group was successful, more land was acquired, and the entire parcel was placed under the care of the Cleveland Museum of Natural History.

In 1966, Mentor Marsh was recognized as a National Natural Landmark by the U.S. Department of the Interior for its value as an example of the natural history of the Great Lakes region. In 1973, 619 acres were designated as a state nature preserve, one of four preserves that were the first in the state to be named.

The marsh is known for its wildlife, particularly migrating birds. As many as 125 different species of birds may be seen or heard on a single day during the spring migration. Migrating monarch butterflies also stop off here. Great blue and green herons, red-headed woodpeckers, wood ducks and red-winged blackbirds have found a hospitable home in the marsh. There are snakes — though no poisonous ones — mink, red foxes, deer, weasels, raccoons, muskrats, beavers and opossums. During the spring, the marsh echoes with the cacophony of spring peepers.

The Marsh House, off Corduroy Road at the southern edge of the sanctuary, serves as an interpretive facility and the starting point for guided hikes each Sunday, spring through fall, at 2:00 p.m. Maps are available for self-guided hikes. Four miles of hiking trails wind throughout the preserve, including the Zimmerman Trail, named after Harold J. Zimmerman, which encompasses the most difficult terrain in the preserve. The .35-mile Wake Robin Trail is built on a boardwalk over the marsh, and takes the visitor among the 12-foot-high reed grass that grows like a solid wall rising from the tea-colored water. The Newhous Overlook is the only portion of the interior that is wheelchair-accessible. A paved path runs a tenth of a mile from the road to a large wooden platform that overlooks the western end of the marsh. The Kerven Trail begins and ends at the visitors' center, winding through forest and meadow, with a stop at the Marsh Overlook. The half-mile School Forest Trail offers an abundant variety of spring wildflowers. While the Marsh House is open only seasonally, on weekends, hiking trails are open from dawn until dusk year-round.

Hikers are advised to wear long pants and carry insect repellent, since trails are often bordered by thorns and burrs, and mosquitoes are an integral part of the marsh ecosystem.

Mentor Marsh State Nature Preserve, 5185 Corduroy Road, Mentor, OH 44060; 440-257-0777.

Headlands Beach State Park

Head out to the Headlands on a weekend in mid-summer and

you'll find a beach full of sunbathing bodies and a lake churning with splashing kids. This is the largest and the nicest beach on Ohio's shore, and it doesn't go unnoticed by the Northeast Ohioans who will happily drive however long it takes to get here. But go during the week, and you'll see a calmer scene — a few young children building sand castles, people reading under the shade of an umbrella, a sailboat or two in the distance. Or spend a fall day walking the mile-long beach alongside the cottonwood trees just beginning to change colors.

The water here can be glass-smooth or ocean-rough, depending on the lake's mood. Although the underwater contour changes a bit every year (sometimes there are sandbars; sometimes there aren't), it generally slopes gradually. There are no strong currents to worry about, and during the summer months lifeguards are on duty.

There are rest rooms and concession stands, as well as picnic tables and grills in a shaded area close to the parking lots.

It's a pleasant walk along the beach through Headlands Dunes State Nature Preserve just east of the park. If you continue on, you can walk out on the breakwall (carefully — the rocks are uneven) to the Fairport Harbor Lighthouse.

Headlands Beach State Park, 9601 Headlands Road, Mentor, OH 44060; 440-257-1330.

Headlands Dunes State Nature Preserve

Just east of the state park, this area of sand dunes is one of last of its kind along the Ohio shoreline. The 16-acre preserve is home to a variety of plants that are unique in their ability to withstand the harsh conditions present on the shore. Extreme heat, scorching sun and high winds are among the adversities these species must contend with. Many plants, such as sea rocket, beach pea, seaside spurge, beach grass and purple sand grass, migrated thousands of years ago from the Atlantic Coastal

Plains, and are not found further inland in Ohio. Although they once flourished along the coastline, beach "improvements" have nearly eliminated them altogether. Other plants in the preserve not commonly found in northeastern Ohio include Canada wild rye, wafer ash, wild bean and switchgrass.

Switchgrass and beach grass are responsible for the dunes' growth. After the grasses become established, sand deposits around them, and the grasses continue to grow, always keeping above the sand that becomes steadily higher. The dunes are supported by the root system of the grasses, which reaches deep below the surface. Further inland, the area is forested by cottonwood, willow and black oak.

Butterflies are common in the preserve, especially monarch butterflies during their migration. Fowler's toads, native to Ohio, are also found here. A small pond has been dredged among the dunes, and it is hoped that it will attract turtles and other aquatic animals and plants.

Although there are no trails in the preserve, paths wind among the dunes and vegetation. As these are worn down into the sand, they are blocked off and allowed to regenerate. Visitors are encouraged to keep to the unblocked paths and avoid walking over the vegetation; although these hardy plants can withstand natural adversity, they are vulnerable to human footsteps. Walking along the beach toward the lighthouse to the east offers a nice view of Fairport Harbor. Occasional interpretive walks are available.

As in all of Ohio's preserves, picnicking, swimming, organized sports, and pets are prohibited.

The preserve does not have its own entrance, but is accessed from the far eastern parking area of Headlands State Park at the end of State Route 44. Rest rooms and water are available at the park.

Headlands Dunes State Nature Preserve, State Route 44; 440-257-1300.

Watching the geese from an overlook in Conneaut.

Lakeshore Reservation

This 86-acre reservation, located on Lockwood Road near Perry, was once the location of ten private homes, the largest of which belonged to Charles Irish, an arborist. The rhododendrons he planted on the eastern boundary of the park are still there, and look oddly out of place among the native trees.

The last parcel of land was acquired by Lake Metroparks in 1973, and the area developed as a park because it is the best example of natural shoreline and mature tree growth along the shoreline in Lake County.

Unlike the teeming public beaches farther east, this is a peaceful, quiet place. A paved path runs from the parking lot through the woods on the eastern side of the park, with a stairway that leads down to the water. The western part of the park is primarily meadow, traversed by a grassy path that winds through the tall vegetation.

The Strock Memorial, in the reservation, was dedicated in 1978 in honor of Luanna Strock, wife of the park's first naturalist, Don Strock. The memorial consists of large stone sculptures, a sculpted sundial designed by Ohio artist Carl Floyd, a bronze cast of the area, and a wooden cable bridge over a ravine in the woods.

Arcola Creek Estuary

It's hard to believe, when you stand on the observation deck overlooking Arcola Creek Estuary, that this was once the site of a bustling town. Yet during the early 1800s, that's exactly what was here. In 1812, bog iron was discovered nearby and soon after Arcole Iron Works was founded. At one time it was the largest industry in Ohio, employing some 2,000 men. Forging iron stoves, kettles and other necessities, the foundry was a large force in the economic life of Ellensburgh, located at the mouth of Arcola Creek where present-day Dock Road ends at the lake.

Today, the creek's mouth is so shallow that it's difficult to imagine ships docking here, but at one time Ellensburgh was not only a port used for shipping and receiving, it was the site of a shipbuilding industry until the last ship was launched from the Bailey Shipyards in 1863. According to the sign posted near the parking lot, "during the early 1800s more ships were built and launched from this port than any other on Lake Erie." Along with the foundry and shipyards, the city boasted a lighthouse, post office, boarding house, grist mill and shops.

By mid-century, the bog iron was nearly gone, the timber used to fuel the foundry fires was depleting rapidly, and the harbor was a victim of shifting sandbars. The town was doomed. Today there's barely a visible trace of what was once there. The 42 acres around the creek and estuary are home to migrating birds. The water serves as a spawning ground for steelhead salmon. The Arcola Creek Estuary owes its present state to the efforts of the Nature Conservancy, the Cleveland Museum of Natural History and the Friends of Arcola Creek. It is managed by Lake Metroparks.

Geneva State Park

Just west of the resort town of Geneva-on-the-Lake, 698-acre Geneva State Park offers camping, boating, swimming, hiking, picnicking, and fishing in the summer; cross-country skiing, snowmobiling and ice fishing in the winter; and hunting in season.

The park's sizable marina, which was completed in 1989, has 383 slips serving seasonal dock holders and transient boats. The concession area meets boaters' needs, including supplies, food and gasoline. Bicycle and wave runner rentals are available. The marina can also offer information on local fishing charters.

West of the marina there's a small but pleasant swimming beach which is guarded in the summer months. Rest rooms and picnic areas are nearby.

The park has several options for overnight guests. A semi-circle of cabins offers a choice view overlooking the lake. These have living, kitchen and sleeping areas and can accommodate up to six people. Reservations are a must, since the prime location makes them quite popular. Reservations are accepted beginning in January each year.

Those who prefer camping will find a fully equipped campground with electricity, showers and flush toilets. The park has three Rent-A-Camp units that provide a tent and other basic equipment for those who want to give camping a try but don't have all the accouterments necessary. These also must be reserved.

Golfers will find a privately-owned public golf course within the park just east of the camping area.

Three miles of trails wind through the woods and by ponds in the area between Padanarum Road, where the park office is located, and State Route 534.

Geneva State Park, PO Box 429, Padanarum Road, Geneva, OH 44041; Park Office, 440-466-8400; Marina, 440-466-7565.

DIVERSIONS

Hach-Otis State Nature Preserve

Located one mile east of Willoughby Hills on U.S. Route 6, this 80-acre preserve offers a spectacular view of the Chagrin River Valley. Two loop trails beginning at the parking lot wind through forest and around deep ravines. The edge of the bluffs overlooking the valley is unstable, so extreme caution is advised. Stay on the trail and away from the rim. Unusual plants in the preserve include trailing arbutus, pink moccasin flower and red trillium. The area is inhabited by white-tailed deer, foxes, raccoons, great horned owls and pileated woodpeckers.

Kirtland

Drive through this small town and you'd swear you were in a New England village. There's plenty of history here in Kirtland, where the followers of Joseph Smith, Jr., built the first house of worship for the Latter Day Saint movement. The Kirtland Temple, dedicated in 1836, is open to visitors. The Church of Jesus Christ of Latter-day Saints also owns and operates the nearby Newel K. Whitney Store and Museum, a restored 1830s country store and post office.

Other restoration efforts have focused on the Mooreland Estate, also in Kirtland. This elegant mansion, owned by millionaire railroad owner Edward W. Moore, was a summer home and place for entertaining. Eleanor Roosevelt and pianist Ignace Paderewski were once guests there. The house is on the grounds of Lakeland Community College.

The Holden Arboretum, just outside Kirtland, is the largest arboretum in the United States. There are 3,100 acres of natural woodlands, horticultural displays, gardens, ponds, fields and trails. The arboretum is open year-round, with special highlights that vary with the seasons. The 20 miles of trails are used for hiking in the spring, summer and fall months, and for cross country skiing in the winter. There is an admission charge.

For more information about Kirtland area attractions, contact the Lake County Visitors Bureau at 1-800-368-LAKE or 440-354-2424.

Lake Metroparks

In addition to its lakefront properties, Lake Metroparks oversees a variety of parks and preserves throughout the county. Chapin Forest Reservation, off State Route 306 near Kirtland, has 390 acres of mature woodland traversed by a network of trails, including a portion of the Buckeye Trail. On a clear day, Lucky Stone Loop offers a panoramic view of Lake Erie and downtown Cleveland, 18 miles to the west. During the 1800s, a quarry operated in what is now the park. Stone quarried here was used to build the Kirtland Temple.

Penitentiary Glen Reservation, on Kirtland-Chardon Road is so named for the deep gorge that cuts through the park. Like a penitentiary, says local lore, it's easy to get into but hard to get out of. Several trails wind through the 360-acre property. There's also a nature center with a gift shop and a wildlife center where injured animals are rehabilitated for release back into the wild. Some animals that cannot be returned to their natural habitat have become permanent residents of the center, providing a look at Ohio's native species.

Lake Farmpark, on Euclid-Chardon Road, near Kirtland, is a unique open-air museum and park that focuses on agriculture. You can milk a cow, discover hydroponics, take a horse-drawn wagon ride or learn everything there is to know about tomatoes. There is a restaurant and gift shop. Each August the park hosts "Vintage Ohio," the state's only wine festival. Lake Farmpark is open all year. For more information about any of the Lake Metroparks call 1-800-669-9226 or 440-256-PARK.

Unionville

Shandy Hall, one mile east of Unionville on State Route 84 (440-466-3680), is virtually frozen in time. What makes this house/museum so special is that it remained in the same family from the time it was built in 1815 until it was bequeathed to the Western Reserve Historical Society. The original furnishings that belonged to the Harper family are still there, including their clothing, farm tools and books. Of special interest is the banquet room with its still-vibrant hand painted French wall paper from the early 1800s. Guided tours are offered May through October, every day but Monday.

A trip to Shandy Hall offers a good excuse to stop off at The Old Tavern (Route 84 at County Line Road in Unionville; 1-800-7-Tavern or 440-428-2091) for lunch or dinner. This old stagecoach stop, built in 1798, was once a part of the Underground Railroad. Today it is a comfortable and picturesque restaurant. The home-made corn fritters, swimming in their little dishes of maple syrup, are well worth the drive.

Wineries

Though not on the lake, two area wineries are an easy drive inland. Chalet Debonne (7743 Doty Road, Madison; 440-466-3485) produces wine from both vinifera and hybrid grapes, including Chardonnay, Chambourcin, Vidal Blanc and Cabernet Sauvignon. The tasting room offers wine and snacks Tuesday through Saturday, year-round. Ferrante Winery and Ristorante (5585 State Route 307, Geneva; 440-466-VINO), is a full-service restaurant serving Italian cuisine and Ferrante wines. Winery tours are also given. Wines run the gamut of vinifera selections such as Chardonnay to those made from native grapes such as Catawba. Wine can be purchased seven days a week, but the restaurant schedule varies, so call ahead to check on food availability.

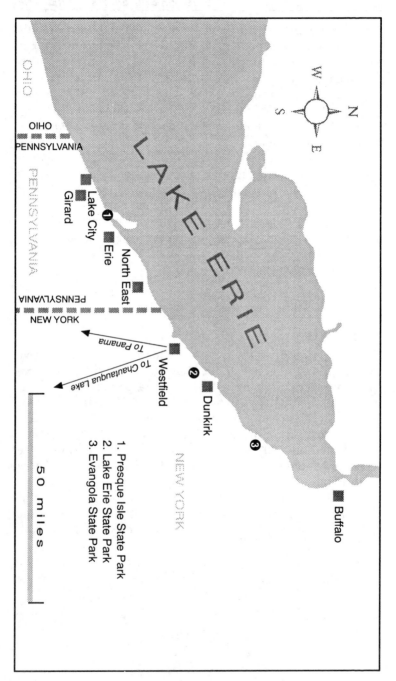

LAKE ERIE

OIHO

OIHO
PENNSYLVANIA

Girard
Lake City
❶
Erie
North East

PENNSYLVANIA

PENNSYLVANIA
NEW YORK

To Panama

To Chautauqua Lake

Westfield

❷
Dunkirk

❸

NEW YORK

Buffalo

1. Presque Isle State Park
2. Lake Erie State Park
3. Evangola State Park

N
W — E
S

50 miles

Chapter *Four*

Pennsylvania and New York

Grape Heaven

In 1869, in a New Jersey kitchen, a discovery was made that would have a profound and lasting impact on the southeastern shore of Lake Erie. After much experimentation, Dr. Thomas B. Welch, a dentist, arrived at a method for making "unfermented grape juice," in his opinion a vast improvement over the alcoholic variety used for communion services. Dr. Welch's small business gradually grew, and he turned it over to his son, Charles, also a dentist. In 1892, the Welch Grape Juice Company was born. Grapes were shipped from New York State to New Jersey for processing into juice until the family decided that a processing plant in New York would be more practical. A facility was built at Watkins Glen.

The Welchs, apparently, didn't do their homework, for they soon expressed dissatisfaction with the location. There were plenty of grapes in the area, but the wrong kind. Concord grapes, which are the only variety used for Welch's grape juice, simply weren't grown in any abundance near Watkins Glen.

Thomas and Charles set about looking for a new location. One look at Westfield, New York, in the heart of Concord country, and they were sold. They negotiated to buy property. That was July 1897. By October of that year, the Watkins Glen plant had been dismantled and the new plant at Westfield was built and equipped. On the 22nd of the month the presses went into action and by November 11, 288 tons of grapes had been processed. By 1902, 1,000 tons of grapes a year were transformed into juice. In 1911, Welch's opened a facility in North East, PA, further widening their sphere of influence.

The grape still reigns supreme in this part of Lake Erie country. While other grape varieties are grown, Concord is the grape of choice for most growers. Most of these are sold to Welch's, while the other varieties supply a small but growing wine-making industry. From just over the Ohio-Pennsylvania border all the way to Dunkirk, New York, vineyards dominate the landscape. In fall, the aroma of sun-ripened grapes fills the air with sweet earthiness to a degree found nowhere else on the lake.

The landscape is different here, too. The water is bordered by high bluffs instead of the marshlands and beaches found on the western American shore. Beaches, in fact, are a rare commodity on this part of the lake, with the notable exception of Presque Isle State Park at Erie, PA. Most of the towns are set inland, where the railroad lines built there in the 1800s aided economic growth. Route 5, which runs along the shore through both states, is almost completely rural until Dunkirk, and is the most scenic drive anywhere on the lake.

Route 5, beginning in Pennsylvania, is the western section of the Seaway Trail, a 454-mile scenic byway that parallels Lake Erie, the Niagara River, Lake Ontario and the Saint Lawrence River. Trail information booths can be found periodically along the route.

Tourist attractions are of the low-key variety — wineries, a couple of lighthouses and railroad museums, Presque Isle. This is the place to go, not for excitement, but for quiet beauty.

SO YOU WANT TO RIDE AROUND THE LAKE?

Touring the perimeter of Lake Erie by bicycle can be a rewarding experience, but it takes careful planning. Whether you plan to camp or stay at B & Bs or motels, plan your overnight stops and make reservations if possible. Especially during the summer, campgrounds and other accommodations are often full. A further 25 miles or so in a car is no big deal, but on a bicycle at the end of a long day, it's another story.

Be sure to carry plenty of water and some snacks; there are long stretches along the Canadian shore where no provisions are available. Basic bike repair tools and spare parts are also a necessity, since bicycle shops are a rare entity except in the major cities.

Speaking of cities, there are a number of them to negotiate: Toledo, Cleveland, Erie, Buffalo, Windsor and Detroit. The best time to ride through them is early in the morning, before rush hour or on weekend mornings before the traffic gets heavy. None of them is impossible, but get city maps and plan your route carefully.

There are places on the Canadian shore where riding on busy Highway 3 is unavoidable. Again, early morning is the best bet. The road is narrow, and with gravel shoulders, it's not pleasant sharing it with trucks. However, the volume of traffic in Canada is far less than on the American side.

The most dangerous stretch of road on the U.S. shore may be U.S. Route 2 between Toledo and Port Clinton. On the map, it looks tempting — it runs right along the lake. But it is a major thoroughfare with only two lanes. Get a county map and work out a route through rural backroads.

There are two singular challenges for cyclists circling the lake. One is crossing from Detroit to Windsor, or vice versa. There are two ways — the Ambassador Bridge or the Detroit Windsor Tunnel. Neither allows bikes. Call a taxi and make sure they can fit your bike in the trunk and have them take you over the bridge — it's at the south end of Detroit and will enable you to avoid a major part of the city.

The other difficulty is crossing wide Sandusky Bay. The only bridge across, on Route 2, does not permit bicycles. You can get over, in a somewhat circuitous manner, by taking the Neuman Ferry from Marblehead to Kelleys Island, then switching to Neuman's luxury boat, the Emerald Empress, which sails to Sandusky. You'll have to ask about bringing along your bike; it's not a common occurrence on the Empress. For information contact Neuman Cruise and Ferry Line at 1-800-876-1907. If you choose to ride around the bay, you must cut south on Route 19 at Crane Creek State Park, ride to Fremont, then pick up U.S. Route 6, which leads northeast to Sandusky.

Both problems and a lot of mileage can be avoided by cutting off the entire western end of the lake if you take the Pelee Island Ferry from Leamington to Pelee Island, continuing on to Sandusky. But then you can't say you rode the whole lake. It's your choice.

For help planning the American portion of your trip you can join Adventure Cycling, PO Box 8308, Missoula, MT 59807-8308; 406-721-1776. For information and maps of the Canadian portion contact The Ontario Cycling Association, 1220 Sheppard Ave. E., Willowdale, Ont. M2K 2X1; 416-495-4141.

County maps can be obtained from the state departments of transportation listed on the next page. There is usually a small fee.

Michigan Dept. of Transportation
Bureau of Transportation Planning
Intermodal Section
PO Box 30050
Lansing, MI 48909
517-373-9192

Ohio Dept. of Transportation
Map Sales, Room 118
PO Box 899
Columbus, OH 43216
614-466-4430

Pennsylvania Dept. of Transportation
Sales Store
PO Box 2028
Harrisburg, PA 17105-2028

New York State Dept. of Transportation
Map Information Unit
State Compus, Bldg. 4, Rm. 105
Albany, NY 12232
518-457-3555

PLACES

North East

More than 300 years ago, what is now the Pennsylvania and
New York shore of Lake Erie was occupied by the Eriez Indians,
a peaceful people. They stood little chance against the fierce
Iroquois, who killed off most of the Eriez and scattered the rest
long before Europeans came to settle. It is for these lost people
of the southeastern shore that the lake is named.

In 1778, Pennsylvania purchased *"The Triangle,"* the extreme
northwest portion of the present-day state, from the Iroquois for
about $150,000. North East, named for its location within the tri-
angle, was the first town to be settled. Like most of the towns

The grape reigns supreme on this part of the lake.

along the lake in Pennsylvania and New York, North East is located inland, about a mile and a half south from the lake shore.

At one time the waterfront area, known as Freeport, was busy with shipbuilding, commercial fishing and lumber shipping. In 1814 there were 15 or 20 families living by the lake shore. Everyone thought it would become a major port. But, like most other lakeside towns on this part of the lake, Freeport failed to flourish and was overshadowed by its inland neighbor, North East. Today, Freeport consists only of a few houses, a restaurant and a small public beach.

North East, on the other hand, has done quite well for itself. But it couldn't have done so without the grape — Concord, to be exact. While some local farmers experimented with native grape varieties, it was the coming of the Concord grape in the 1850s that really put North East on the map. Ideally suited to the region's conditions, the Concord flourished. Then, when the railroad came through town, the farmers had an easy way to transport their goods. Business boomed.

In 1911, Welch's came to town. Today, it's the largest processor of Concord grapes in the world and the town's primary employer. Every fall at harvest time, the Welch's plant churns out juice 24 hours a day to process the tons of grapes brought in by local growers. One way or another, nearly everyone in the town has something to do with grapes. They're so pervasive that the public school sports teams call themselves the Grapepickers.

But it's not just grape juice that North East is known for; there's also wine. The first winery in the area, the South Shore Wine Company, was founded in 1869. Others soon followed. North East's location on the railroad line made distribution easy, and the industry prospered. Then, in 1918, Prohibition hit and the wineries went under. It wasn't until 1968 and the passage of the Limited Winery Act that commercial wine-making was once again permitted. Today, four wineries draw visitors from all over to sample their wares.

Among the first to open their doors when the new law was passed was Penn Shore Winery and Vineyards (814-725-8688), located on Route 5 east of town. Penn Shore makes wines primarily from native and hybrid grapes. Along with the usual selection of sweet wines such as Niagara and Pink Catawba, the winery also produces some crisp whites — Seyval Blanc, Vidal Blanc and — perhaps their best offering — Vignoles. Tastings in the pleasant tasting room are free. The winery is open every day year-round, with extended hours in July and August.

Just down the road is Mazza Vineyards (814-725-8695), owned by Robert Mazza, who is also part owner of Penn Shore. The winery produces three categories of wines: "table wines," which are of the sweet variety such as Concord; "premium wines," such as Riesling, Vidal Blanc, Chambourcin and Chardonnay; and "specialty and fruit wines" like strawberry, peach and cherry. Among the specialty wines is an icewine made from Vidal Blanc grapes grown on the property. Mazza makes this wine in the traditional way, harvesting by hand in the fall or early winter when the grapes are frozen on the vine and their juice is high in concentrated sugar. The result is a rich, sweet wine that has brought the winery acclaim. A guided tour followed by a free tasting is available year-round.

Mazza Winery in North East, Pa.

Also east of town, but on Route 20, is Heritage Wine Cellars (814-725-8015). The original 100-acre fruit farm was purchased in 1833 by an ancestor of the present owners, the Bostwick family. The tasting room is located in one of the original farm buildings, now 150 years old. Visitors who think to look at the ceiling will no doubt be impressed by the 72-foot beam of virgin walnut that runs the length of the room. Also impressive is the sheer quantity of different wines produced at the winery. They are lined up across the tasting bar where guests can help themselves. From Niagara to Chardonnay to an unusual Almondiera, this winery covers all the bases. They also make a number of red wines, including Concord, Isabella and "Burgundy." Though a great many choices are offered, Heritage does its best job with the sweeter wines. There's a restaurant upstairs with a beautiful view of the lake in the distance. Diners can choose a wine that suits their taste and take it upstairs to enjoy with a meal in the indoor dining room or outside on the deck. A full service menu is available for lunch and dinner. The winery is open seven days a week. Call for restaurant hours.

Winemaker Bob Green (left) and owner Doug Moorehead at Presque Isle Wine Cellars.

The home-made, hand-painted sign on Route 20 announcing the entrance to Presque Isle Wine Cellars (814-725-1314) doesn't look very promising. Neither do the rather cluttered grounds of the winery. But of the four wineries in North East, this is the one where serious wine lovers are likely to find what they're looking for. Doug Moorehead, who owns the winery along with his wife Marlene, was a pioneer in growing European grape varieties in Pennsylvania. A grape farmer since 1956, Doug opened the winery in 1969 and set to work promoting what some thought was impossible. A firm believer in the feasibility of growing vinifera grapes in this region, Doug's efforts have proved more than successful. Under the expertise of winemaker Bob Green, Presque Isle produces a knock-your-socks-off Chardonnay, a delightfully crisp Riesling and a fruity, refreshing Pinot Rose. In an area that rarely produces good dry red wines, Presque Isle excels. The Pinot Noir, Cabernet Sauvignon and Cabernet Franc are all excellent. Grape varieties more common to Pennsylvania aren't neglected either, such as a clean, fruity Cayuga. Prices are very reasonable, especially considering the excellent quality.

Though the winery is frequently busy with its main occupation of selling wine-making supplies to amateur vintners, informal tours and tastings are always available for the interested visitor. The tasting room is bright and cheery, with a deck attached. There are also picnic tables on the grounds, next to a pretty stream. The friendliness of the staff and owners is infectious — this is a place that encourages lingering. The winery is open all year, but closed on Sundays.

In the town of North East, the grape motif is always present. There's the Grapevine Cafe, the Concord Card Shop, and Ye Old Vineyard Crafts and Antiques. The Chamber of Commerce sign bears a cluster of the fruit. It's not a wonder that the most celebrated event of the year is the annual Wine Country Harvest Festival held each year at the end of September. There are tastings and tours at each of the wineries, craft sales, hayrides, grape stomping, a petting zoo and live entertainment. There's also a bike tour through the wine countryside.

Perhaps it's not too surprising, in a town so inclined to enjoy itself, that the first church, established in 1801, was soon converted to a tavern. Or that the first hotel was called the Brawley House.

But any other time of the year, North East is the very picture of propriety and grace. Lovely Gibson Park, in the center of town is a shaded haven with a fountain and benches. Around its edges, beautifully preserved architecture houses a variety of small businesses. The campus of Mercyhurst College, with its broad, grassy lawns and distinguished buildings lies just north of the center of town. The entire downtown area is a designated national historic district. A self-guided walking tour highlighting North East's historical architecture is available from the Erie County Historical Society, 417 State Street, Erie, PA 16501; 814-454-1813.

The Lake Shore Railway Museum (814-825-2724), at Wall and Robinson Streets, is located in the former New York Central passenger depot. In addition to displays of memorabilia and models, there are several train cars on the tracks outside, including a locomotive, dining and sleeping cars, a tank car and three refrigerator cars. Occasionally, the museum runs train excursions complete with on-board dining. Museum hours vary according to the month so call for information. It is closed November until Memorial Day weekend.

Where to stay:

Grape Arbor Inn
51 East Main Street
North East, PA 16428
814-725-5522

This is a very classy place. Guests will find their rooms stocked with plush terry robes, complimentary toiletries, a little box of chocolates and a bottle of local wine. The beds are covered with fine cotton linens and goosedown comforters. The inn consists of seven antique-filled rooms or suites named for local grape varieties, five in the main building and two in the house next door. All are equipped with TV/VCR, air conditioning, telephone and private baths. The suites have working fireplaces; one also has a kitchen. Full gourmet or hearty continental breakfasts are served on the sun porch, outside on the patio or, on cold winter mornings, in the dining room next to a crackling fire. The main building, an 1832 Federal-style brick mansion, has served as a stagecoach tavern, a stop on the Underground Railroad, a boardinghouse, a kindergarten and a restaurant. Owners Kathleen and Robert Mazza (of Mazza Vineyards) and Susan and Donald Moore do not live on the premises, but manager Joy Northup does and can assist guests to make their stay enjoyable.

Where to eat:

Freeport Restaurant
Corner of Rt. 5 and 89
814-725-4607

The Freeport Restaurant may not be much to look at, but it's a great stop for a good home-cooked meal. Owners Jerry and Judy Holdsworth make their own sausage, smoke their own ham and bacon, and slice up their fries from scratch. Sandwiches, salads, stick-to-your-ribs dinners like Southern fried chicken, prime rib, beer-batter fried walleye are the fare here. Homemade soup is available daily. And for dessert save some room there are

Barcelona Lighthouse, just north of Westfield, N.Y.

homemade pies ranging from raspberry to peanut butter, with about a dozen varieties in between.

For more information contact North East Area Chamber of Commerce, 21 S. Lake Street, North East, PA 16428; 814-725-4262.

Westfield

Westfield bears many similarities to its Pennsylvania neighbor, North East. Like North East, Westfield sits back from the lake. Also like North East, its harbor town, which seemed destined for greatness, proved otherwise, while the inland town grew and flourished. And probably most important, Westfield — like North East — makes its living from grapes.

The first white men likely to have set foot on the lake shore near present-day Westfield were the French explorers Robert de La Salle, Father Louis Hennepin and the crew of the Griffon, who, records show, passed through the area in 1679. The French returned in the mid-1700s, when they cleared a trail from the lake shore to the northern tip of Chautauqua Lake. The Portage Trail, as it became known, opened the way for invasion from the north clear to the Ohio Valley, and played a part in the unfolding events that culminated in the French and Indian War.

It wasn't until the early 1800s that settlers arrived in the area. The land was owned by the Holland Land Company, a group of Dutch bankers. They sold off lots, in 100-acre parcels, to pioneers looking for a new life. After a confusing series of land mergers, divisions and the renaming of towns and settlements, Westfield was founded in 1829.

But even before the founding of Westfield, Portland Harbor, as the harbor area was known, was a busy place. Early settlers brought grain and lumber there to trade for the supplies that came in on ships. Warehouses lined the shore and a settlement established itself. Business increased, and in 1827 the federal government declared Portland Harbor a Government Port of Entry. A post office called "Barcelona" was built — a name that would later supplant "Portland Harbor."

Every indication pointed to continued growth. The need for a lighthouse prompted the government to allot $5,000 for construction of a tower and a keeper's cottage, which were completed in 1829. The light crowning the 40-foot tower was lit by oil until a large deposit of natural gas and a "burning spring" were discovered nearby. Wooden pipes were built to span the three-quarter-mile distance from the spring to the lighthouse, and on July 5, 1830, the Barcelona Lighthouse became the first in the world to be lit by natural gas.

Business at Barcelona slumped after 1852, however, when the construction of an inland railroad line made shipping by water less desirable. Ironically, it was the railroad that spurred the growth of commercial fishing at Barcelona because, for the first time, the catch could be moved quickly without danger of spoilage. However, the railroad spelled the end for the shipping industry at the port and by 1855 there was little need for a lighthouse. In 1859, the light was turned off and the property reverted to its previous owner, the Holland Land Company.

The lighthouse still stands guard over Barcelona Harbor, and a gas light has been placed at the top of the tower by the Iroquois Gas Corporation. Even though the lighthouse is no longer used officially for navigation, an "eternal light" still glows from the picturesque stone tower.

With the advent of the Concord grape, Westfield's future was determined. The temperate lake climate and loamy soil made for perfect growing conditions. By 1880 grape-growing was a major industry, aided by the railroad line that made it possible to ship to distant points. In 1897, Dr. Charles Welch and his father came to Westfield and immediately set out to find a site for a processing plant. By harvest season that year, the plant was up and running, using grapes purchased from local growers to produce juice. In 1917, unusually cold weather caused many grapes to freeze, making them unsuitable for juice. Farmers feared a bad year. As it happened, they had nothing to worry about. That was the year "Grapelade" was born, the predecessor of today's American staple, grape jelly.

Welch's is still a major player in the town of Westfield, also known as the *"Grape Juice Capitol of the World."* Grapes, however, also produce wine, and contrary to the wishes of founder Thomas B. Welch, even Welch's began fermenting juice in 1951. Today, two local wineries produce a variety of offerings from local grapes.

The Johnson Estate Winery (716-326-2191), on US Route 20 west of town, is the oldest estate winery in New York State. All grapes used in their wines are grown on their property. You won't find a Chardonnay or a Cabernet lurking on the shelves at Johnson — their wines are produced strictly from native or hybrid grape varieties. It's a bare-bones tasting room that visitors encounter, but tastings are free and available every day, all year.

There's a very different tasting experience to be had at Schloss Doepken Winery (716-326-3636), also off Route 20, especially if owner John Watso is presiding. He lines the bottles up on the counter and tells in a slow, almost-reverent tone the story of each

The McClurg Mansion and Museum, Westfield, N.Y.

wine. He is quite proud of his products, and rightfully so. They range from an oaky Chardonnay to a spiced wine that tastes like liquid apple pie. The Riesling is very good, as are some vintages of Chardonnay; the Gewurtztraminer is also excellent. The winery is less successful with the reds, though an oak-aged Baco may sate the tastes of dry-red lovers. The tastings take place in a gift shop that sells wine-related items. The name of the winery comes from the German word "Schloss," which means "castle of" or "house of," followed by his wife's maiden name, Doepken.

For those who yearn for a taste of something sweet and non-alcoholic, a stop at the Sugar Shack (716-326-3351 or 1-888-563-4324) on Route 5 is a must. Owner Gail Black is a grape-grower who dabbles in fruit syrup on the side (which, for a farmer, means at 5 a.m.). She uses her grandmother's recipes to make fruit syrups and butters from wild berries that grow on her property and fruit that she cultivates, producing flavors like wild currant, wild blackberry, elderberry, raspberry, blueberry, peach and pear — not to mention all the varieties of grapes she grows. She also makes and sells maple syrup.

The first question Gail likes to ask when visitors come through the door is, "Where are you from?" She then marches over to a map on the wall and adds a star on the visitor's hometown. For every year there's a U.S. and a world map; she can pull out the map and show you she had visitors from Tierra del Fuego and South Korea, as well as a dozen or more European countries. Following a "syrup tasting," Gail takes guests on a walk over a trail that runs down to the lake, pointing out native tree species, wild flowers and fruits along the way. In 1996 the Sugar Shack won a Seaway Trail National Trails Day Award for "land related resources."

Downtown Westfield is distinguished by stately old homes and mansions. One of these, the McClurg Mansion, has been made into a museum. The building that is now the McClurg Museum (716-326-2977) was begun by James McClurg in 1818. Newly married, McClurg wanted to provide a comfortable life for his family, and so he set about building a 16-room mansion the likes of which had never been seen in the town before. "McClurg's Folly," the townspeople called it — surely a cabin would do. McClurg persisted, baking his own bricks and preparing the lumber himself. Two years later the home was completed. It remained in the McClurg family until 1936, when the last heir died and left it to the Village of Westfield. It has been a museum since 1951. The house is filled with antiques and fine art from the collection of the Chautauqua County Historical Society, which operates the museum. Particularly striking is the hand-carved mahogany ceiling with grape motifs installed by McClurg's daughter in the 1870s. Hours vary, so call before visiting.

Antique hunters will find plenty to occupy themselves in Westfield. The town is known for its quality antiques shops that line Main Street and extend out to the countryside. Furniture, glassware, china, oriental rugs, jewelry, lamps, books and clocks are just some of the items that can be found while browsing through town. A list of the shops and their specialties is available from the Chamber of Commerce.

Westfield does not have a public beach, but there is a pleasant park overlooking the lake. Ottaway Park, located on Route 5 east of Barcelona Harbor, has a grassy picnic area with tables and a great view. An admission fee is charged.

Where to stay:

Westfield House
PO Box 505 (E. Main Road)
Westfield, NY 14787
716-326-6262

It took Betty and Jud Wilson many years to find the perfect house in which to open their B & B. They found it in Westfield — an 1840 farmhouse in the Gothic Revival style. Each room has a private bath and most are air-conditioned. A pantry area is provided for guests who would like to keep beverages or snacks cold. The elegant living room has a TV/VCR and a selection of tapes. A side porch makes a pleasant place for coffee in the morning or reading in the afternoon. Betty and Jud serve a full breakfast that includes home-made baked goods and a hot entree such as eggs benedict or pancakes.

The William Seward Inn
South Portage Road, Route 394
Westfield, NY 14787
716-326-4151

In 1991, Jim and Debbie Dahlberg took a deep breath and plunged into the inn business. They came from quite different backgrounds. Jim had been in the banking business in Buffalo for 30 years. Debbie had been a fair housing advocate. But it was their dream to have an inn, especially one where Jim could share his considerable cooking talents with guests. They bought the William Seward Inn, an 1821 Greek Revival mansion named after one of its previous owners who had been Secretary of State under Abraham Lincoln. Under their ownership, the inn has become one of the most notable places to stay on Lake Erie. There are 13 guest rooms — nine in the main building and four luxury rooms with Jacuzzi baths in what was once the carriage house. All rooms have private baths and air conditioning. All are tastefully decorated with antiques. Some of the rooms have gas fireplaces or balconies. There is a living room for guests as well as a library with TV/VCR. One of the most memorable features of the inn is Jim's cooking. Four-course dinners to suit the most epicurean tastes are offered every Wednesday through Sunday nights (see "Where to eat" following). Gourmet breakfasts are served to guests each morning and are included in the price of the rooms. This is the perfect place for a special romantic get-away.

Where to eat:

Barcelona Harbor House
Barcelona Harbor (end of Route 394)
716-326-2017

Sunsets over the lake can be spectacular at the Barcelona Harbor House, which offers a completely unobstructed view of the water. The casual eatery isn't much to look at from the outside, but the inside is cozy and comfortable. Specialties are seafood dishes, including lake perch and walleye, though beef-eaters and chicken fans aren't ignored. Vegetarian items are also available. Prices are reasonable and the food is quite good. There's a pleasant bar decorated in a nautical theme.

The William Seward Inn
South Portage Road, Route 394
716-326-4151

If you don't stay at the William Seward Inn, make it a point to have dinner there. You'll find such delights as Portobello Mushroom Napoleon, Filet of Beef with Ginger-Soy Butter Sauce or Medallions of Veal with Calvados Cream, all prepared with care and skill by inn owner Jim Dahlberg. The prix fixe menu, which changes every couple of months, includes appetizer, salad, entree and dessert with coffee or tea. A nice selection of wines is also available. Diners must make reservations and are asked to make dinner selections in advance. Dinner is served Wednesday through Sunday nights. During the summer there are two seatings; the rest of the year there is one. Dinner at the William Seward Inn can only be described as intimate, romantic and elegant. Leave the kids at home and have a fling.

For more information contact the Westfield Chamber of

Commerce, PO Box 25, Westfield, NY 14757; 716-326-4000.

Dunkirk

When Dunkirk was founded in 1805, it went by the name of Chadwick Bay. It was renamed in 1817 after Dunkerque, France, because of the similarities of the towns' harbors. The people of Dunkirk have always had more than a nominal connection totheir sister city: at Thanksgiving, 1946, the citizens of Dunkirk shipped $100,000 worth of emergency supplies to their war-torn namesake.

Unlike most other towns on this part of the lake — the noted exception being Erie, PA — Dunkirk is blessed with a large protected harbor, which made it a suitable center for shipbuilding, fishing and commerce. For ship captains caught in an angry lake, Dunkirk offered the only real refuge between Erie and Buffalo. Unfortunately, what must have been a beautiful sight then is today less than attractive, with industrial clutter marring the aesthetics of the lakefront.

Although within the grape belt, Dunkirk grew to be an industrial town, not an agricultural one. The graceful tree-lined streets and well preserved architecture of Westfield and North East just aren't found here. But even though Dunkirk is not nearly as appealing as its handsome neighbor to the south, Fredonia, it has a truly distinguishing treasure in its lighthouse.

Dunkirk Historical Lighthouse and Veterans Park Museum (716-366-5050), located on Lighthouse Point Drive off Route 5, is one of the few Lake Erie lighthouses that can be toured. The brick keeper's house and adjoining tower were built in 1875 at Point Gratiot, the site of a previous lighthouse that had been built in 1827. The new Fresnel lens alone cost $10,000, a hefty sum at the time.

While the light itself continues to be operated by the U.S. Coast Guard, the keeper's house has been turned into a museum. The downstairs rooms are furnished as they might have been when the keeper lived on the premises. A passage connects the house

Ong-Gue-Ohn-Weh, Dunkirk, N.Y.

with the tower. On dry days it is possible to climb the cast iron winding staircase to the light, 82 feet above the lake surface.

The second floor of the keeper's house is given over to displays of military memorabilia from World War I through Desert Storm. A separate building houses artifacts primarily from the Coast Guard. On the grounds are various anchors, a lighthouse buoy tender, a rescue boat and several buoys. The lighthouse and museum are open daily in July and August, less frequently other times. It is closed January through March.

Just west of the lighthouse grounds is Point Gratiot, a 75-acre public park with bathing beach, large grassy picnic area with shelter, a playground, a short bike trail and a nature trail.

A strange sight greets the traveler on the north side of Route 5 east of Point Gratiot. Ong-Gue-Ohn-Weh, a wooden sculpture of an Indian, sits in an unfortunate location next to the water treatment plant. Carved in 1973 by artist Peter Toth, it is a monument to the American Indian. Ong-Gue-Ohn-Weh means "The Indian" in the Seneca language. The artist hopes to erect similar statues in each of the 50 states.

At the Dunkirk Historical Museum (716-366-3797), a half-mile south of Route 5 at 513 Washington Avenue, visitors can learn about the history of the area. Exhibits include displays on local businesses, schools and individuals. The Canon Leslie F. Chard Library on the premises houses local histories, maps and books by local authors. The museum and library are open noon to 4 p.m., Monday through Friday.

The museum also sponsors the ALCO-Brooks Railroad Display at the Chautauqua County Fairgrounds in Dunkirk during June, July and August. The display features the Boston and Maine #444 locomotive, built at the American Locomotive Company's Brooks Works in Dunkirk in 1916. The display also includes a 1907 wooden box car, a 1905 caboose and many smaller artifacts.

Canadaway Creek Nature Sanctuary, on Temple Road on the west side of town, is a small parcel of land owned by the Nature Conservancy. Though most of it is woods south of the lake, a small part of it is on the lake and is one of the few remaining sections of undeveloped lake front in New York. There are two unmarked trails with excellent examples of native plants and trees.

No town in grape country would be complete without a winery. Dunkirk's contribution to the New York wine scene is Woodbury Vineyards Winery (716-679-9463), on Roberts Road south off Route 20. Owner Gary Woodbury represents the third generation of his family to grow grapes on this property. Most of the acreage is planted with Concord grapes, which Gary sells to Welch's. The remaining couple of acres are planted with Chardonnay, Riesling and Cabernet from which the winery produces some very good wines. They also make wines more common to the area, such as Seyval Blanc and Niagara. A unique program called Adopt-a-Barrel allows patrons to pay a set fee for a winery barrel, to which a plaque with their engraved name is attached. At the end of a four-year waiting period, the barrel is theirs — along with two cases of wine. Tours and tastings are available daily throughout the year. There are picnic tables on the grounds, making this a pleasant place for a luncheon stop on a bright autumn day.

While visiting Dunkirk, take the time to drive south a bit to the adjacent town of Fredonia. At its center is the New England-style Barker Commons, featuring two ornate Victorian cast iron fountains. The commons is framed on all sides by Fredonia's beautiful architecture — fine examples of Greek Revival, Gothic, Victorian and other styles.

Where to stay:

White Inn
52 E. Main Street
Fredonia, NY 14063
716-672-2103

Though not close to the lake, the White Inn offers the most unique accommodations in the area. This impressive, pillared building was constructed in 1868. There are 23 guest rooms or

Canoeing in Grave Yard Pond, Presque Isle State Park, Pa.

suites, some with fireplaces or Jacuzzi baths. The rooms and public places are furnished with antiques and period reproductions. The on-premises restaurant enjoys considerable acclaim.

For more information contact the Dunkirk Chamber of Commerce, 212 Lake Shore Dr. W., Dunkirk, NY 14048; 716-366-6200; or the Fredonia Chamber of Commerce, 5 E. Main Street, Fredonia, NY 14063; 716-679-1565.

NATURAL ATTRACTIONS

Presque Isle State Park

Jutting seven miles into Lake Erie, this 3,200-acre park is the crowning glory of the American shore. In a part of the lake where there are almost no beaches, Presque Isle has nearly seven miles of them. There are also ponds, lagoons, wooded trails, protected bays for fishing and nearly six miles of paved multi-purpose trails. Some of the most beautiful sunsets seen on the lake are from the beaches on Presque Isle.

Presque Isle is not an island, but a peninsula connected by a narrow strip of land to the mainland just west of Erie, Pennsylvania. The French named the place *"Presque Isle,"* meaning *"almost an island,"* though it has actually been an island at times when storm waves separated the peninsula from the mainland.

The narrow strip of land at its base gradually widens as it curves to the northeast. At its farthest point, it nearly touches the mainland seven miles east of the base, creating a vast body of water called Presque Isle Bay.

Offering the only protected harbor on the Pennsylvania shore, Presque Isle was recognized as something special long before the French named it. According to an Eriez Indian legend, a group of their people paddled far into the center of the lake to see where the sun set every evening. Instead of finding the sun, they were faced with one of the lake's devastating storms. The Great Spirit saw their plight and raised his left arm into the lake to offer them protection. A sandbar formed where his arm had been, creating a permanent refuge.

It was a refuge of sorts for Sailing Master Daniel Dobbins and Master Shipwright Noah Brown during the spring and summer of 1813. Charged with building the American Lake Erie squadron during the War of 1812, they produced two 480-ton brigs and three smaller schooners from local oak, pine, cedar and black walnut, all within the protected waters of a small inlet off Presque Isle Bay.

In August, the fleet sailed out of the bay and on to victory in the western basin of the lake, under the command of Oliver Hazard Perry. Perry and his men returned to Presque Isle in case of further British attacks. Their refuge became a trap that winter, as many succumbed to smallpox and were quarantined to the bay. Their bodies were buried in what is now known as Grave Yard Pond. The small, protected inlet where the fleet had been built and where the men later suffered and died was christened Misery Bay. In 1926 the Perry Monument, a 101-foot Indiana limestone structure, was built at the site.

The beach at Presque Isle State Park, Pa.

Presque Isle has a unique natural history as well. There are six distinct ecological zones in the park, each supporting different species of plants and wildlife. Among the most numerous inhabitants of Presque Isle are birds. The area is a major resting spot for migrating birds because of its location beneath the Atlantic flyway, one of the invisible *"freeways in the skies"* that birds follow instinctively. More than 320 bird species have been observed here, including many that are rare or endangered.

The prime periods for observing waterfowl are in March and late November through December. Shore birds are most prevalent in April and August. Warblers make their appearances in mid-May and again in September.

Gull Point, a 319-acre sanctuary at the extreme eastern point of the peninsula, is a particularly good place to spot migrating shore birds, hawks and land birds. Although 67 acres of the sanctuary are off limits to visitors from April 1 to November 30, there is an observation tower that looks out over the restricted area that is accessible from a trail beginning at Budny Beach.

The first stop for visitors should be the Stull Interpretive Center near Barracks Beach shortly beyond the park entrance. Park personnel are on hand to answer questions, and maps and other printed information are available. There are exhibits depicting the formation and evolution of Presque Isle as well as the birds, plants and animals that are found there. The Nature Shop in the center sells field guides, nature books and other nature-related items.

Beaches are a prime attraction for the thousands of visitors who flock to Presque Isle in the summer months. There are so many beaches that even on a gorgeous summer weekend they aren't likely to be crowded. Most of them are found along the lake shore of the peninsula, where wave action provides fun for older children. However, young children (and their parents) may be happier at Beach 11, which is tucked into a protected area between the main part of the peninsula and Gull Point. The water is very calm here and the bottom slopes quite gradually. Beaches 6, 8, 10 and 11 have rest rooms, changing facilities, and food and beverage concessions. Beaches 1 and 9 have rest rooms and changing facilities but no concessions. The rest of the guarded beaches are close to rest rooms. Beach 7 has a ramp that provides wheelchair access to the water's edge. Beaches are open 10 a.m. to 8 p.m. Memorial Day weekend through Labor Day. Swimming is permitted only at designated beaches when lifeguards are on duty.

The park's marina has 500 slips that can accommodate boats up to 42 feet in length. The marina season runs May 1 through October 31. For those who wish to launch their boat in the park, there are four ramp areas that can accommodate different sized crafts. Boats with internal combustion engines are not permitted in certain parts of the interior lagoons.

Several types of boats, including canoes and small powerboats, can be rented at the livery on Grave Yard Pond. From the livery it's possible to take a canoe, rowboat or electric boat through the interior lagoons and ponds for a close-up look at one of the park's many habitats. Pontoon boat rides through the lagoons with a naturalist are available from Memorial Day through Labor Day.

Visitors can tour the bay or the lake around Presque Isle on the Lady Kate, a large powerboat that can accommodate up to 49 people. Tickets can be purchased at the Lady Kate's berth in Misery Bay near the Perry Monument. The Appledore, an 85-foot topsail schooner, offers bay sails from its port in downtown Erie. For information and reservations call 814-459-8339.

Fishermen will appreciate the abundant crappie, pike, bass, perch and walleye found in the area. Early spring brings small-mouth bass season, when it's not unusual for anglers to hook a four- to seven-pound catch. Muskies are caught from spring through fall. Winter cold doesn't stop fishermen at Presque Isle, where ice fishing is a popular activity.

There are many types of picnic facilities available, from individual tables to covered shelters with electricity and running water. Tables and grills are scattered throughout the park. Picnic pavilions can be reserved; those that aren't taken are available on a "first come, first served" basis. A large cookhouse with enclosed cooking area, electricity and water is located at about the middle of the peninsula. The cookhouse can accommodate up to 200 people. There are also three enclosed shelters nearby with electricity, water, tables and fireplaces. These must be reserved by calling the park office.

There are 16 hiking trails in the park totaling approximately 13 miles. The longest of these is 2.25 miles, but many trails intersect, making it possible to plan longer hikes. Trails are clearly marked on maps available at the Stull Interpretive Center. Hiking the trails is an excellent way to observe the varied habitats of the park: shoreline, sand plains, dunes, ponds, marshes, thickets and forests. During periods of high water, parts of the trails may be wet or submerged. Deer ticks are found in the park, so proper clothing and precautions are advised. The 5.8-mile multi-purpose trail is the only trail open to cyclists and skaters. Its smooth, well-maintained surface makes it ideal for these purposes. The trail runs from the park entrance to the Perry Monument.

Presque Isle is open year-round. In winter, the portion of the multi-purpose trail from the park office near the entrance to the

The Appledore sailing at Presque Isle State Park.

Perry Monument is available for cross-country skiing. Other winter activities include hiking, ice fishing, ice skating and ice boating on Presque Isle Bay, Misery Bay and the marina area.

While the park is for day-use only and has no cabins or camping, there are many motels near the park entrance. One of the most pleasant of these is the Beachcomber Inn (814-838-1961), on West 6th Street at Peninsula Drive. Another popular attraction in the area is Waldameer Park and Waterworld (814-838-3591), a family amusement park only a few minutes' drive from Presque Isle.

For more information on Presque Isle State Park contact the park office at Box 8510, Erie, PA 16505-0510; 814-833-7424.

Lake Erie State Park

Located on Route 5 between Barcelona and Dunkirk, this 355-acre park is one of the oldest state parks in New York. Shortly after the park entrance on Route 5, the park road arrives at a toll booth where admission is charged. One road then leads off toward a picnic and beach area, the other to a campground.

The picnic area is on a grassy, shaded area that slopes down to a small beach. On either side, high bluffs overlook the water. There is a bathhouse with changing facilities. Fishing is permitted from a jetty to the west of the beach. A 1.5-mile loop hiking trail, one of two in the park, leads from the parking lot toward the east end of the park property. The picnic area has tables and a covered pavilion with barbecue pits.

The camping area, accessed from the other road, has 97 campsites and 10 semi-primitive cabins. The view of the lake from the cabins is especially beautiful. The campsites are unshaded and in an open area. Most have electricity, but not all. There are shower and toilet facilities at the campground, as well as a playground and miniature golf. The other hiking trail, for which there is an interpretive guide, runs west of the campground. During the winter the trails are open to cross-country skiers.

For more information contact Lake Erie State Park, R.D. #1, Brocton, NY 14716; 716-792-9214.

Evangola State Park

On Route 5 about halfway between Dunkirk and Buffalo there's a sign announcing the entrance to Evangola State Park. The drive down the long, wide entrance road seems to take forever. With the manicured lawns and grassy median, you could just as easily be approaching an antebellum mansion as a state park. But finally the road ends at the lake, where there is a large bathhouse and a small beach. Picnic areas crown the bluffs on either side of the beach. Tall trees offer plenty of shade, and there are many tables and several shelters. Rest rooms are also found here. Grills are provided, but no garbage containers — picnickers are expected to carry their trash out. If the beach is perhaps less appealing than those found west in Ohio or at Presque Isle, the overall setting and the picnic area with its lovely view of the lake make this a worthwhile stop.

The other primary use of the 745-acre park is by campers. There are 82 sites, some of which have electricity, in the campground which is west of the beach and picnic area. Tennis courts, basketball courts and laundry facilities are available for campers.

Park services, including lifeguards, are provided on weekends beginning Memorial Day until the last weekend in June, then daily until Labor Day. Other times, the park may be open for walkers (there are quite a few paved walkways), but swimming is forbidden when there is no lifeguard on duty.

For more information contact Evangola State Park, Route 5, Irving, NY 14081; 716-549-1760.

DIVERSIONS
Girard/Lake City

The neighboring towns of Girard and Lake City are a few miles inland approximately halfway between the Ohio-Pennsylvania border and Erie, Pennsylvania. Girard had its heyday in the mid-1800s, when the Extension of the PA Main Line Canal connected it with Erie. From 1845 until the canal's closing in 1871, the town prospered. With the canal's closing came an end to the growth, and today Girard is a small, quiet town. It is also the location of an interesting group of museums known collectively as the Battles Museums of Rural Life, operated by the Erie County Historical Society.

The museum complex is named for Rush S. Battles, a banker who began business in Girard in 1859. The R.S. Battles Bank, which financed much of the area's growth, was the only bank in the region during most of the 19th century. At the Battles Bank Museum, visitors can see much of the original bank equipment such as the safe and teller's cage. Other exhibits change periodically.

The Orientation Center for the museum is at the First Universalist Church of Girard, built in 1867. The congregation of this church, which is still active, was involved with the

Underground Railroad during the Civil War era.

The Battles Farmhouse, built by Rush Battles in 1857-58, housed his mother and two unmarried sisters until their deaths. In 1989 it was renovated for use as a museum. The first floor of the rural Italianate home houses changing exhibits, while the rest of the house is used for the museum staff.

Just down the road is the Charlotte Elizabeth Battles Memorial Museum, the house that Rush and his wife Charlotte built for their family. Their daughter, Charlotte Elizabeth Battles, who took over the family business, lived in the house until her death in 1952. The house still contains the Battles' family possessions. An exhibit tells the story of the Battles family, giving insight on what it might have been like to live in this rural area during the 19th century.

The Battles Museums Ecology Trails, located on approximately 80 acres of woodlands, are used to teach visitors about the plants and animals indigenous to the area and how they may have affected the lives of the early settlers.

Tours can be designed to suit interests and physical capabilities. For information about the Battles Museums contact the Erie County Historical Society at 417 State Street, Erie, PA 16501; phone 814-454-1813. The society also publishes a self-guided walking tour booklet of Girard.

On your way back to the lake shore, stop at Lake City for a meal at the All Aboard Dinor (yes, it's really spelled that way — a western Pennsylvania anomaly) in the old passenger train depot in the center of town. If a train rumbles by, your water will jiggle in its glass and you won't be able to hear your partner, but you'll sure get a close-up view.

Chautauqua Lake

It's only about a 15-minute drive from Westfield, New York, to the northern tip of Chautauqua Lake. Route 394 from Westfield takes you right into Mayville, where you can take a ride on the

All Aboard Dinor at the old Lake City depot, Lake City, Pa.

Chautauqua Belle, one of only three working paddlewheel steamers east of the Mississippi. Continuing down the western side of the lake, the road passes the world-renowned Chautauqua Institution, where every summer the lakeside comes alive with concerts, plays, opera and lectures. About midway down the lake, you can drive across the bridge on Route 17 to Bemus Point, a delightful small town with good restaurant and interesting specialty shops. Or you can take the Stow-Bemus Point Ferry, an antique vessel that shuttles passengers, cars and bicycles across the lake May through September. If you continue to the southern tip of the lake you'll come to Jamestown, home of the Lucy-Desi Museum, the Roger Tory Peterson Institute and the Jamestown Audubon Nature Center. On the east shore is Long Point State Park, a 320-acre day-use park with swimming, picnicking, hiking trails, cross-country skiing and snowmobiling. For more information about the Chautauqua Lake area contact Mayville/Chautauqua Area Chamber, PO Box 22, Mayville, NY 14757; phone 716-753-3133.

Panama Rocks Scenic Park

Located at Panama on Route 10 southwest of Chautauqua Lake, the boulders, crevices, passageways, caves and dens at Panama Rocks are the result of glacial movement over what was once a vast salt ocean. In addition to the geologic formations, the park is noted for its mosses, ferns and wildflowers. There is a one-mile, self-guided hiking trail for which good footwear and a flashlight (for seeing into dens and crevices) are recommended. A snack bar and picnic area are provided, though the snack bar is open limited hours. The trails pass by deep crevices and there are no fences, so parents are cautioned to watch children closely. Visitors are required to sign a waiver. This privately-owned park was established in 1885. For more information call 716-782-2845.

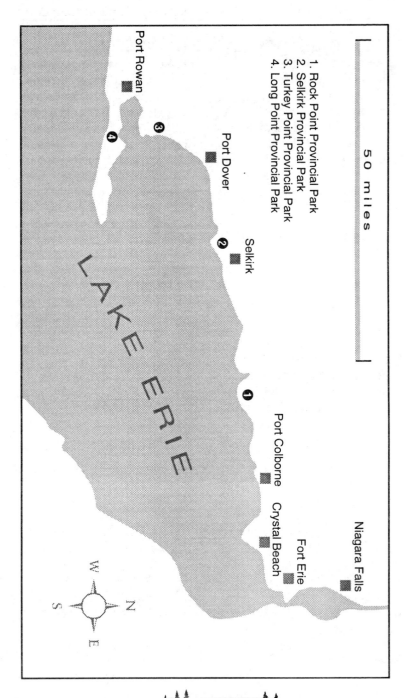

50 miles

1. Rock Point Provincial Park
2. Selkirk Provincial Park
3. Turkey Point Provincial Park
4. Long Point Provincial Park

LAKE ERIE

Port Rowan

Port Dover

Selkirk

Port Colborne

Crystal Beach

Fort Erie

Niagara Falls

N W E S

Chapter _ive_

Eastern Ontario
A Change of Scenery

A sk an American from Cleveland or Erie what's on the other side of the lake and you might just get a blank look. Many have ventured no further than Cedar Point or Presque Isle. Yet the Canadian shore is a traveler's delight. Eastern Ontario boasts Fort Erie, with its many historical sites; Port Colborne, at the entrance to the Welland Canal; Port Dover, home — at least in spirit — to the foot-long hot dog and endless summer fun; and Port Rowan, perched at the north end of the longest sand spit on Lake Erie. Accommodations, while less plentiful than on the American side, are generally more economical, as are food and attractions. The dollar — whether Canadian or American — stretches a great deal farther here on the north shore.

Perhaps the most stunning view of the lake is the one encountered while driving over the Peace Bridge from Buffalo to Fort Erie. To the right, the Niagara River rushes toward Niagara Falls, where it will tumble 170 feet at the rate of 34 million gallons per minute. To the left is the broad, blue expanse of the eastern edge of the lake, framed on one side by the skyscrapers of Buffalo and on the other by the grassy parks of Fort Erie.

This contrast between bustling American cities and pretty Canadian towns is one that characterizes the entire lake shore.

Aside from Fort Erie, which owes its importance primarily to its strategic location at the lake's far eastern corner, and Port Colborne, which earned a dot on the map only after the Welland Canal was built, the towns of the Canadian shore are sleepy fishing villages that awaken only during the summer months with the influx of Canadian tourists and "day-trippers."

Why the difference? While the Americans were busy dredging harbors to accommodate the lucrative trade in iron ore and other riches of the industrial age, the Canadians were setting down roots and planting fields. Their interest was not in the lake, but in the fertile land along its shores. Ports the size of Sandusky or Ashtabula simply weren't needed, and so they never developed. What trade there was took place inland, over a network of rail

---

PSST! IT'S A SECRET — THE BEST SHOPPING

Everyone loves a unique shop and there are plenty of them in these places:

In Ridgeway's historic shopping district you can buy handmade pottery at The Art of Pottery (401 Ridge Road), stock up on English cheeses, jams, teas and other items at Adams English Shop (193 Ridge Road), quench a chocolate-lover's desires at The Chocolate Outlet (309-311 Ridge Road), stock up on candles, folk art and country-themed items at Country Bunny Gifts (411 Ridge Road) or buy Victorian-inspired treasures at Lasting Impressions Gifts (356 Ridge Road). On Port Colborne's West Street, you'll find Brigadoon (158 West Street), which sells an intriguing combination of children's clothing, hand-crafted gifts and unique furniture upholstery; Crew's Quarters and Captain's Cabin (192 West Street), purveyors of brass antique reproductions, pewter, candles, garden statues and windchimes; and a host of other clothing shops, bakeries and restaurants. In Port Dover, Dolls and Friends (20 Market Street) offers 2,500 square feet of exclusive collectable dolls, stuffed animals, framed prints and other gifts.

A staff member in period costume gives a tour to visitors at Historic Fort Erie.

road lines and roads, and it was along these routes that the major Ontario towns such as London and Simcoe grew. The ports — Port Dover, Port Maitland, Port Ryerse and others — were home to fishing fleets and a modest ship building trade, not host to the giant freighters the likes of which were often seen at Conneaut or Lorain on the Ohio shore.

What the north shore lacks in commerce and industry is more than made up for in charm and natural beauty. Miles of farmland, long sandy beaches, pretty port towns, quaint shops, fish restaurants overlooking the water — these are the things that await the traveler to Canada's shore.

PLACES
Fort Erie

Fort Erie, with it 26,000 inhabitants, is the most populous town on the Canadian shore and has the feel of a border town. Buffalo residents have long flocked to Fort Erie and the beaches beyond for entertainment and relaxation. The Fort Erie Racetrack, in operation since 1897, draws thousands annually. On weekends, the streets of the town are filled with cars bearing New York license plates, and U.S. currency flows as freely as Canadian.

In fact, Buffalo and Fort Erie are so friendly toward each other that each year they have a Friendship Festival. Taking place at the end of June and beginning of July, the two-week festival combines celebrations of Canada Day (July 1) and the Fourth of July, with events such as concerts, fireworks, car shows, competitions and craft demonstrations, held on both sides of the river.

There was a time, of course, when there was neither an American nor a Canadian side. It was during this era, in 1764, that a fort was built by the British and named Fort Erie. It was the first fort built on the shores of the lake and was considered a remote outpost, infested with snakes and mosquitoes in the summer, bitterly cold in the winter.

Built too close to the water, the fort fell victim to one of the lake's vicious storms and was destroyed. It took another fort, another storm and another destruction before the British figured out that higher ground might make more sense. Construction of a new fort in a better location began in 1805. It had not been completed when war broke out between Great Britain and the United States in 1812. The British abandoned the fort; the Americans moved in and then left. The British occupied again, and for a month, beginning in August, 1814, the fort was the site of a full-scale siege in which many lives were lost. In November that year, American troops retreated to Buffalo, destroying the fort as they departed.

It was left in ruins until 1937, when reconstruction was begun, sponsored by the Provincial and Federal governments and the Niagara Parks Commission. Today it is a major tourist attraction that draws many to its picturesque location overlooking the lake. Historic Fort Erie (905-871-0540) is open mid-May to mid-September. Admission includes a guided tour of the fort, showing the officers quarters, the soldiers' barracks, the kitchen and the powder magazines. The staff, in period costumes, illuminate the daily lives of soldiers as they might have been during the 1812-1814 period.

Each year there are several special events at the fort. In June, King George III's birthday is celebrated. Every August, the 1814 siege is re-enacted, complete with tactical displays. But the event that's closest to Fort Erie citizens' hearts is the annual Loch Sloy Highland Games, held each year at the end of June.

Fort Erie has the second highest concentration of people of Scottish ancestry in North America (the highest is Fergus, Ontario), and they take it seriously. During the games, the drones of bagpipes and the rhythmic taps of drums are mingled with the cheers of spectators watching kilted men competing in traditional Scottish athletic events. There are pipe band competitions, step dancing demonstrations and storytelling sessions. You can sample Scottish foods, buy Scottish goods and listen to Scottish ballads.

Brought about by a bizarre series of events, the Irish also had considerable influence over the Fort Erie area. In 1866, approximately 1,300 disgruntled Irish-American veterans of the Civil War, who called themselves the Fenian Brotherhood, launched a plan to march into Canada, lay siege, and force the British to relinquish control of Ireland. Amazingly, they expected the Canadians to cheer their efforts to "liberate" Canada. This would seem to be a vast misjudgment of character, since most of the mothers and fathers of Fort Erie's residents had been Loyalists who fled from the south rather than live in the new, renegade country.

Early in the morning of June 1, the Fenians crossed the Niagara River and the invasion began. For the next two days, battled raged between the troops commanded by the Irish-American, General O'Neill, and Canadian forces. The Fenians fought well, but the reinforcements they waited for never arrived. They were forced to retreat back to Buffalo.

Today, the route and events of the battle can be traced along the Battle of Ridgeway Scenic Drive, using a self guided tour prepared by the Fort Erie Museum Board. At the Ridgeway Battlefield Museum (905-894-5322), visitors can tour a cabin that once stood on the edge of the battlefield. Built in the early 1800s, the cabin, now filled with artifacts of the era, was inhabited by

A bagpiper at the Loch Sloy Highland Games, held annually at Historic Fort Erie.

John Teal and his family when the invaders arrived.

A remarkable series of paintings depicting the battle can be seen at the Fort Erie Historical Museum (905-894-5322). Alexander Von Erichsen, an obscure painter, followed the Fenians from Buffalo into Canada and recorded the events he witnessed. The resulting paintings were lost, and only recently resurfaced in a Virginia attic. Fortunately, the museum was able to bring them to Fort Erie, where they are on permanent display. Other displays include artifacts from the native inhabitants of the area, and memorabilia of Crystal Beach Park, an amusement park that flourished nearby for nearly a hundred years before its closing in 1989.

The third municipal museum of Fort Erie is the Fort Erie Railroad Museum (905-871-1412). There visitors can climb aboard a 94-foot locomotive and tour a 1944 caboose. Two old railway stations have been moved to the museum site. The Ridgeway Station, built in 1910, served the village of Ridgeway

A cruise ship passes through the Welland Canal at Port Colbourne.

until 1975. The bright, airy building includes a waiting room and telegraph office filled with artifacts of a time when travel was still pursued with leisure. The B-1 Station was once located at the Canadian side of the International Bridge that spans the Niagara River. Its sister station, B-2, was on the American side. Built in 1873, the building's exterior has been restored. It houses the admissions desk, a small gift shop and the museum office.

The three municipal museums are open seasonally. The Battlefield Museum and the Historical Museum are open mid-June through Labor Day; the Railroad Museum is open mid-May to mid-October. Visitors can purchase a pass which entitles them to admission at all three museums.

Two private museums in Fort Erie are also worth a stop. The Mildred M. Mahoney Doll's House Gallery (905-871-5833) is located in Bertie Hall, a Greek Revival mansion on the banks of the Niagara River. Under its roof is the largest collection of doll houses in the world. Like many girls, Mildred Mahoney spent a good portion of her childhood playing with dolls. They lived in an orange crate, the most luxurious accommodation her family could afford. A visit to the Million Dollar Castle, a doll house owned by actress Colleen Moore, inspired in Mildred a life-long dream to own such a doll house. It wasn't until adulthood that her dream came true. She began collecting doll houses and never stopped. There are doll houses from Japan, England, Europe, Canada and the United States, decorated down to the tiniest fine detail. Mildred even upholstered the furniture in antique fabrics and sewed lace curtains to line the miniature windows. The museum is open May to December.

At the Fort Erie LaFrance Association Museum (905-871-1271), visitors can see fire-fighting equipment dating from the 1860s. There's a 1947 American LaFrance and a 1952 60-foot ladder truck. The museum, which was begun by volunteers from the Fort Erie Fire Company Station No. 2, is open July through Labor Day.

Just west of Erie is the village of Ridgeway for which the famous battle with the Fenians was named. The historical section of Ridge Road is now a quaint shopping district, with gift shops, a creamery, clothing stores and even a British import shop.

Southwest of Fort Erie, and nearly a suburb of it, is the small, quiet town of Crystal Beach. It wasn't always so quiet. In 1888, John Evangelist Rebstock bought a parcel of beachfront here with the intention of selling the sand to a Buffalo construction company. But he couldn't help noticing the crystal clear water and fine sand. He had a better idea. He would turn it the area into a religious assembly ground with a few attractions on the side. Human nature being what it is, the attractions were more popular than the religious programs, and Crystal Beach Park was born.

Gradually, excursion boats began to run between Buffalo and Crystal Beach. The Canadiana was the largest of these, capable of carrying 3,500 passengers. Families came in the evenings and on the weekends to ride the park's miniature railway, aerial swing and merry-go-round, and to bowl, skate at its rink and dance in the pavilion. In 1924, ground was broken for what would be one of the largest dance halls in North America. Big names like Glenn Miller, Stan Kenton and Les Brown came to play. In 1927, the Cyclone took its first passengers. Billed as the "largest, fastest, safest and most thrilling ride," this 96-foot-high roller coaster nonetheless was staffed with a nurse at the unloading platform for the 20 years it was in operation.

Throughout its history, however, the park was plagued with financial problems. Though it changed ownership several times, no one seemed to be able to turn a profit consistently. It closed its gates on Labor Day, 1989. Despite the efforts of local citizens to ensure that the land would remain accessible to the public, the new owners built a private club. Today, the old haunt of summertime revelers is occupied by the Crystal Beach Tennis and Yacht Club. There is a public beach just to the west, where the water still lives up to its name.

The town maintains some of it holiday character, though the closing of the park has brought hard times. But with its powdery sand and exceptionally clear water, the beach is still one of the prettiest on the lake, and makes for pleasant walk by the dock that once brought thousands for a day or evening of fun.

Where to stay:

Crystal Beach Motel
122 Ridgeway Road
Crystal Beach, Ontario L0S 1B0
905-894-1750

For a town the size of Fort Erie there's a surprising dearth of interesting places to stay. Even the large chain hotels have not found their way here yet. But a pleasant throwback to the days of "mom and pop" motels can be found outside Fort Erie in the small town of Crystal Beach. The rooms at the Crystal Beach Motel are large and newly remodeled, each with air-conditioning, TV and fridge. There are picnic tables, grills, a playground and a pool that owners Doris and Henk Post keep meticulously clean.

Where to eat:

Black Creek Restaurant and Tavern

A hot dog stand at Port Dover.

660 Garrison Rd.
905-871-2444

Every evening finds Black Creek owner Shirley Ennis going from table to table chatting with her guests and checking that everything is just as it should be. She greets everyone who comes in and wishes all a good day or evening as they go out. It's not unusual for Shirley to remember a visiting guest from the previous year. But Shirley's warmth isn't the only reason to go to the Black Creek Restaurant and Tavern. Try good food, generous portions and reasonable prices, in a casual, friendly atmosphere. It's an eclectic menu, with the likes of cabbage rolls, barbecued ribs, and Lake Erie walleye rubbing shoulders with oriental stir-fry and vegetarian lasagna. Then there're the desserts — like apple caramel walnut cheesecake, chocolate raspberry truffle and white chocolate mousse. Go, enjoy, and leave the calorie counter at home.

The Pines Restaurant
3990 Erie Road
Crystal Beach

Sightseers embark on a tour of the Lynn River at Port Dover.

905-894-3269

You won't find anything even remotely resembling gourmet food here. What you will find is hearty, stick-to-your-bones cooking — things like steak, pork chops, liver, ribs and filet of sole served up with salad, mashed potatoes with gravy, and unadulterated vegetables. Surrounded by tall pines and lined with pine paneling, the restaurant is reminiscent of Crystal Beach's past as a lake resort. The building was, in fact, the site of Reickert's Tea Room, a popular place in the 1930s.

For more information contact the Fort Erie Chamber of Commerce, 427 Garrison Rd., Fort Erie, Ontario L2A 1P1; 905-871-3803.

Port Colborne

Port Colborne is a working town, one that owes its existence largely to the Welland Canal. Although Pennsylvania Mennonites settled in the area in the early 1800s, it was the opening of the canal through to Port Colborne in 1833 that spurred the growth of the town. What was once an obscure section of lake shore was now host to ocean-going ships on their way from the St. Lawrence Seaway to the upper Great Lakes. The canal allowed a way around what was once conceived of as an invincible obstacle — Niagara Falls. Over a distance of 26 miles, the new system of locks enabled vessels to navigate the 326-foot difference in sea level between Lake Ontario and Lake Erie. Ship chandlers, blacksmiths, merchants and tavern owners established businesses to accommodate the ship traffic, and even today much of the town's commercial activity is related to the canal.

New canals were built in 1853, 1887 and again in 1932, reducing the number of locks from 40 to eight. Remnants of the old canals can still be seen to the west of the present canal in Port Colborne.

It is the canal that first greets visitors approaching Port Colborne from the east. Highway 3 passes over a lift bridge just above the Welland Canal Lock 8. Fountainview Park, a well-maintained municipal park, overlooks the lock, which is the last one ships traveling west must pass through before entering Lake Erie. Ships sailing to Lake Ontario have a 12-hour journey ahead before leaving the last of the locks at Port Weller. It is an impressive sight to watch behemoth ships maneuver into the relatively narrow lock.

Closer to the lake the canal passes West Street which is lined with historic buildings, including the first brick commercial structure in the town. Built in 1850 by the Carters, a prominent Port Colborne family, it served as a grocery and later as a general store and post office. Today, it is Gavin's Men Shop, one of many specialty shops, galleries and restaurants that make West Street Port Colborne's most picturesque commercial area.

A glimpse of Port Colborne's rich history can be seen at the Historical and Marine Museum (905-834-7604) on King Street downtown. The museum, which consists of several buildings and attractions, is on the property originally owned by John and Maria Williams. The house was built in 1869 and remained in the family until Arabella Williams donated it and the land to the city in 1950. The house is the main part of the museum, with exhibits depicting development of the canal and marine history of the area. Other buildings include the carriage house, which is now a gift shop; and a rental cottage, which is now Arabella's Tea Room. Every afternoon June to September, volunteers serve tea, homemade biscuits and jam. There are also two log structures — a log house typical of the Pennsylvania Mennonite settlers and a log schoolhouse, thought to be among the first schoolhouses in the area. A blacksmith shop, a wheelhouse from a steam tug and a restored 1949 lifeboat complete the museum attractions. It is open daily from May to December.

On a hot summer's day, residents flock to Nickel Beach, located east of the canal. The wide, sandy beach stretches along the lake, bordered by wooded sand dunes. Though open to the public, there is an admission fee, since the beach is owned by INCO, a refinery that produces nickel, cobalt and other metals.

The other prime lakefront gathering spot is H. H. Knoll Lakeview Park, located at Sugarloaf Harbour on Gravelly Bay west of the canal. The park, with its wide, grassy expanse, overlooks the Sugarloaf Marina and the huge towers of the Maple Leaf flour mill. The park is used for picnics and fishing, frisbee-throwing and just plain walking. On special days and holidays it's the site for concerts and other gatherings.

Sugarloaf Harbour Marina, located adjacent to the park, hosts a variety of events during the spring through summer months, including an Ice Breaker Regatta in May, followed by weekly sailboat races, fishing contests and regattas.

The town's Showboat Festival Theatre offers light-hearted theater in the round, with each seat no more than 20 feet from the stage.

Every summer Port Colborne celebrates Canal Days, a weekend filled with food, entertainment, crafts, games and contests held at H.H. Knoll Lakeview Park, on scenic West Street, at the Historical and Marine Museum and at Nickel Beach.

Where to stay:

Grace's Victorian Lodging
77 Kent Street
Port Colborne, Ontario L3K 2Z6
905-835-8037

For years, Grace Bennett worked with senior citizens. She enjoyed them so much she opened a lodging house especially for seniors. When the four bedrooms aren't occupied with her senior friends, she opens them up to B & B customers. Her lovely home is decorated in Victorian decor, and includes a fireplace in the living room. The baths are shared. There's a large dining room where breakfast is served. Grace will also prepare home-cooked dinners upon request.

A CANADIAN RESORT

Sherkston Shores, between Fort Erie and Port Colborne, is the only full-scale resort on the Canadian side of the lake. There are 2.5 miles of sandy beach, swimming pools, mini-golf, a waterslide, hiking and bike trails, tennis courts — the list goes on. There's plenty of space for tent camping or RVs, but those who prefer a holiday home will find those too. They vary from small units with no air-conditioning to large, air-conditioned luxury homes with a lake view. For more information contact Sherkston Shores, R.R. #1, Empire Road, Sherkston, Ontario L0S 1R0; 800-263-8121.

Ingleside
322 King Street
PortColborne,
Ontario L3K 4H3
905-835-5062

When she was in her twenties, Sandi Paterson hitchhiked through Europe and had an awakening. While she was enjoying tea in the dining room of a B & B in London the proprietress, Miss Sinclair, asked, "What do you want to do with yourself?" Sandi looked at the elegant furnishings surrounding her and said, "I'd like to have a B & B." "And so you shall," Miss Sinclair answered. It was a long time coming, but Sandi got her wish. Ingleside, Sandi's B & B, was built in 1867 for the Carter family, who lived in it for 118 years. Port Colborne's first mayor, Dewitt Carter, was one of its residents.

Sandi and her husband, Brent Bisnette, have turned it into a gracious B & B with two air-conditioned guest rooms, each with full bath. The carefully restored house is decorated with antiques; the grounds include a garden, courtyard, fish pond, and the original smoke house and ice house. It's within walking distance to the museum and the historic West Street shopping area.

Rathfon Inn
815 Lakeshore Rd. W.
Port Colborne, Ontario L3K 5V4
905-835-2399

The Rathfon Inn isn't in Port Colborne, but four miles west on the lake shore. It's secluded and tranquil — the perfect place for a retreat. For that reason, the Inn is popular among groups who need a quiet place for a weekend meeting, but individuals are also welcome. The original house was built in 1797 by Mennonite settlers and was an inn from its beginnings, with two rooms for the family and two to let out. What was once the carriage house is now a large meeting room. The two original buildings have since been joined under one roof and two floors of guest rooms have been added (there are 18 of them). The Inn is situated on nine grassy acres overlooking the lake. Guests are served home-made croissants with home-made jam for breakfast. There is a heated pool on the property.

Where to eat:

The Upper Deck
3 Marina Drive
905-834-9991

This is without a doubt the most scenic location for dining in Port Colborne. Located at Sugarloaf Harbor, the Upper Deck has a great view of the lake, the lighthouse and the marina. The best bet here is fresh lake perch or walleye.

Sugar's Too
10416 Lakeshore Rd.
905-834-0586

Located west of town in a quiet rural area, Sugar's Too is a small,

The original mill built by John Backhouse in 1788.

casual restaurant overlooking a fish pond and garden. The fare is simple but good — perch, steaks, walleye or chicken followed by homemade pies such as rhubarb custard or peanut butter cream.

For more information contact the Economic Development Office, City of Port Colborne, 239 King Street, Port Colborne, Ontario L3K 4G8; 905-835-3361.

Port Dover

The route from Port Colborne to Port Dover is mostly rural, with cottages lining the lake and farms inland. The road passes through Dunnville, just north of the shore, over a bridge across the Grand River. If you continue on the inland route to Port Dover, you'll drive past miles and miles of farmland — the fact that the 1996 International Plowing Match was held here is a telling bit of trivia. If you chose the shoreline route — which can be done except for a few short sections — it's slow going along the twists and turns that follow the water's contours. Approaching Nanticoke, still a few miles east of Port Dover, you are greeted by a strange and incongruous sight — dozens of electrical towers fanning out from a power plant, followed by the futuristic towers of a steel mill and oil refinery — all surrounded by plowed fields and little else. Shortly thereafter, Route 6 bears down into the town of Port Dover, a lively and picturesque community at the mouth of the Lynn River that attracts families and fun seekers throughout the summer months.

The first white visitors to what is now Port Dover were two French priests exploring the region with the intent to bring religion to the native people. Dollier and Galinee arrived at the spot in the fall of 1669, just as the weather began to turn. They built a cabin and spent the next five months in the place of which they said, "there is assuredly no more beautiful region in all Canada."

Dollier and Galinee had more than religion on their minds, however. They wasted no time before claiming the land for France. In their proclamation, "Act of Taking Possession of the Lands of Lake Erie," they wrote that they "had taken possession in the name of their King, as of an unoccupied territory, by affixing his arms which they have attached here to the foot of this cross." While the original cross has long since vanished, the spot is still marked.

Less than a hundred years later Lake Erie, so confidently declared French, was granted to Britain with the signing of the Treaty of Paris in 1763, but settlers were a long time coming. After the American Revolution they began to trickle in, many of them Loyalists from New York State and New Jersey who came to farm the rich land at the edge of the lake. A mill and later a saw mill and distillery were built close to where Port Dover is today and the settlement that grew up around them was called Dover Mill.

Then the War of 1812 broke out. The Canadian mills became strategic targets for the American army, since they supplied flour for British troops. Lt. Col. John Campbell prepared to sail across the lake from the American side and destroy them. He landed at Dover Mill and ordered the burning of the town. An

American private later had this to say: *"In a short time the houses, mills and barns were all consumed, and a beautiful village, which the sun shone on in splendor that morning, was before two o'clock a heap of smoking ruins."* Campbell defended his actions by saying that he had merely retaliated for similar acts the British had perpetrated toward the Americans, but a Court of Inquiry conducted by the U.S. Army subsequently condemned him for the burning of private homes.

After the war, Port Dover, as it was then called, turned once again to agriculture, while developing the fishing and shipbuilding industries for which it later became famous. Until relatively recently Port Dover was the home of the largest fishing fleet on the Great Lakes. While fishing still plays a part in the economy of the town, tourism and the industry at nearby Nanticoke have replaced it as the mainstay.

Port Dover may have had its origins in the serious business of survival, but today it's a town bent on having a good time. Near the beach are old fashioned hot dog and ice cream stands, beach shops and souvenir stores. Main Street is lined with antique and gift shops, boutiques and cafes. There are miniature golf courses and Jet Ski rentals. On a summer afternoon, the long, sandy beach is crowded with sunbathers, picnickers, kids splashing in the water and people playing volleyball.

The place to start is the tourist information center on Market Street, where the staff can provide information about local attractions, including boat charters and excursions. The information center also serves as ticket office for the well-known Lighthouse Festival Theatre (519-583-2221) next door, which produces plays and musicals throughout the summer season.

Just outside the tourist center, and at several other locations in town, visitors can board the "Dover Rover," a tram that travels through the town while a guide provides commentary.

The Port Dover Harbour Museum (519-583-2660), at the pier on the river, provides some historical background on the area. Built as a net shanty in 1947, the small wooden building has been a museum since 1977. There are displays that relate to the fishing industry nets, floats and indigenous fish and other maritime topics.

A favorite spot to view the lake is from the pier that juts out from the mouth of the Lynn River. Every evening in good weather, families stroll its length to the lighthouse at the end. Benches along the way make a good spot to stop and enjoy the sunset.

Just outside the business district at the end of Main street is the beginning of the Lynn Valley Trail, a five-mile hike and bicycle trail that runs northwest, linking Port Dover to Simcoe. The trail follows a rail line that was abandoned in 1988. There are picnic tables and benches along the gravel path. For information and a map contact the Lynn Valley Trail Association, 137 Decou Road, Simcoe, Ontario N3Y 4K2; 519-428-3292.

Every Sunday evening in July and August there are free live band concerts in the gazebo at Powell Park, a grassy, pleasant expanse in the center of town. Each year in July, the town also sponsors the annual Fish Fest. The third weekend in August brings the annual Summer Festival, when antiques and arts and crafts are displayed at Powell Park.

At the Port Dover Harbour Marina, on the east side of the Lynn River, visitors can charter a sailboat or cruiser for fishing, sightseeing or sunset cruises.

Port Dover may not have the historical attractions of a town like Fort Erie or the cultural attractions of a big city. What it does have is family fun — lots of it.

Where to stay:

Bed and Breakfast by the Lake
30 Elm Park
Port Dover, Ontario N0A 1N0
519-583-1010

Christine and Peter Ivey have been welcoming guests at their ranch-style home on a bluff overlooking the lake since 1993. There are two guest rooms and one shared bath. A brick patio makes a pleasant spot for coffee in the morning or watching the lake late in the evening. A small sandy beach is just 100 yards from the house. Christine serves home-made muffins and jam with seasonal fresh fruit, along with omelets and toast for those who like a more substantial breakfast. What draws people back again and again to the Bed and Breakfast by the Lake is the warmth of Christine and Peter, who have a natural knack for making their guests feel at home.

The Port of Call

Box 106
602 Main Street
Port Dover, Ontario N0A 1N0
519-583-1642

Built in 1855 by Walker Powell, the son of Port Dover's founder, this large Victorian home is more than just a B & B. It is also the residence and studio of internationally-known artist Lanny Horne and his wife, Lynda. The main floor and common living areas serve as a gallery for Lanny's colorful paintings, while the converted attic is his studio (Interested guests are often invited up for a tour). The beautifully decorated air-conditioned house features single, double and family rooms with shared baths. Children over 12 are welcome. There is a patio with outdoor fireplace and fish pond surrounded by gardens where guests can enjoy Lynda's home-cooked breakfasts. The Port of Call is open year-round.

Brant Hill Inn

30 John Street & Highway 6
Port Dover, Ontario N0A 1N7
519-583-1501

This European-style hotel has 12 deluxe rooms with TV, telephone, mini-fridge and full bath. There's also a sauna and whirlpool. Breakfast is served either in the dinning or on the patio. It's away from the bustle of the town, but close enough to walk to. Reasonable rates, large comfortable rooms and a distinctive feel make Brant Hill different from the ordinary motel.

Where to eat:

Erie Beach Hotel
Walker Street
519-583-1391

The Erie Beach is an establishment of sorts in Port Dover. It opened its doors in 1946 and many things about it haven't changed since. One of them is the excellent perch — some of the best to be found along the lake. A unique item of fare is the freshly baked celery bread, served with every meal. Be sure to change from your shorts and T-shirts — the Erie Beach isn't necessarily dressy, but beach clothes aren't appropriate.

The Gingerbread House Restaurant and Tea Room
19 St. Andrew Street
519-583-0249

This is undoubtedly the only place in town where you can dine on Ontario Ostrich or Buffalo Bourguignon. For more Plebeian tastes there's lamb and halibut with papaya sauce. Whatever you have at the Gingerbread House, you can count on it being carefully prepared. According to the restaurant's "statement of purpose," the staff is "dedicated to the use of the highest quality fresh ingredients, locally produced if at all possible, not adulterated by adding any additives or preservatives." The luncheon menu includes salads, soups, croissant sandwiches and desserts like gingerbread cake with creme fraiche or Georgian pecan cake. At the time of writing, the restaurant had not yet gotten a license to serve alcohol, but plans are underway.

For information contact the Port Dover Board of Trade, Information Centre, Box 239, Port Dover, Ontario N0A 1N0; 519-583-1314.

Port Rowan

The lake road from Port Dover to Port Rowan is primarily rural, passing through the tiny hamlets of Port Ryerse and Fisher's Glen, the larger village of Normandale and the beach town of

Twins Ice Cream Parlour on Main Street in Port Rowan.

Turkey Point. Of these, Turkey Point is probably of the most interest to visitors. The focal point is the beach, a long, sandy affair that stretches the length of the town and is part of Turkey Point Provincial Park. Opposite it are snack shops, ice cream stands, a couple of motels and an arcade. It's a great place to spend a day.

A few miles to the west the road arrives at Port Rowan, a small town whose commercial district is only a couple of blocks long. What Port Rowan may lack in size, it makes up for in spirit. It's an upbeat little place — you just have to look at the local newspaper, the "Port Rowan Good News," to see that. There are no grim tales here. The headlines read "Summer is here!" and "Peregrine falcons, bald eagles make recovery." Each year Port Rowan holds is annual Tomato Fest, a family-oriented event that includes a parade, street dance, fireworks, entertainment, amusement rides, food and more.

Downtown is pleasant, with its ice cream parlor, coffee shop and fish and chips restaurant, but most visitors come to see two attractions that are just outside the village.

One of these is Long Point, just to the west, a peninsula of sand and wetlands that extends more than 20 miles into the lake, creating a large bay that shelters Port Rowan and the surrounding area. The point is well-known as a stopover for migrating birds in the spring and fall, and also for its many species of turtles. It may be the only place along the lake where turtle crossing signs are posted.

Long Point not only hosts a number of different natural environments, it bears varying degrees of impact by humans. Unfortunately, the upper part of the peninsula is more developed than may be expected; there are campgrounds for RVs, cottages, stores and snack bars. But the road also passes the Big Creek National Wildlife Area, where numerous species of waterfowl can be spotted. There's a trail that follows along the marsh, about a 45-minute walk.

Farther down the peninsula is Long Point Provincial Park *(see Natural Attractions)* and then the Long Point Company, a private hunting club that has been overseeing and protecting this part of the peninsula since the government sold the land to the club in 1866. The club's land is inaccessible to the public. Beyond is the Long Point National Wildlife Area, a protected parcel of land also inaccessible except for very small portions that can only be reached by boat. It is ironic but understandable that the photos often seen of Long Point — long stretches of dunes, undisturbed vegetation and a picturesque lighthouse — cannot be seen by the casual visitor, who instead sees primarily cottages, trailers and the typical beach shops. The best time to visit Long Point may be in the spring or fall when the area is not so congested with campers. These are also the best times for viewing the migrating birds. Those interested in birds may wish to contact the Long Point Bird Observatory (519-586-2885) about bird banding demonstrations during the migration periods.

Long Point has a long and colorful history. Because it extends so far out into the lake, it effectively cuts the lake's width in half, making navigation difficult. Like a spider in its web, Long Point has been trapping unlucky ships since the beginning of navigation on the lake. Crashed onto shore during storms or heavy fog, more than 175 ships have met their demise in the lake's most populous graveyard.

The Atlantic was one such victim. The sidewheel steamer was rammed one night in 1852 by another steamer, the Ogdensburg, in the narrow passage around Long Point. On board were 550 to 600 people, many of them Norwegian immigrants headed, they thought, for a new life. Unaware that there had been serious damage, the Ogdensburg sailed on. Not until they heard the screams of the drowning did the crew turn back. In confusion and panic, many of the passengers leaped from the Atlantic only to be crushed by its paddlewheels. Many of the Norwegians could not understand English and therefore couldn't follow instructions for evacuating the ship. The Ogdensburg picked up as many survivors as it could, but two thirds of the passengers perished in 160 feet of cold, dark water.

A strongbox containing $35,000 — a lot of money in those days — also went to the bottom. Attempts to locate it were never successful, though many have tried over the years. One of the more ingenious attempts was made by Lodner D. Phillips, who invented the first submarine ever used on the Great Lakes. He was above the wreck of the Atlantic in 1864 when the submarine broke loose and sank, where it now rests next to the old steamer. Fortunately, Phillips was not on it at the time.

All such places must have a ghost story or two, and Long Point is no exception. One November night a steamer got into trouble off the point. Knowing that the ship was a loss, the captain steered it toward shore, hoping to save the crew. While lowering the lifeboat, one of the crew was accidentally decapitated. Although the remaining crew searched for the missing head, it was never found and they had to bury their shipmate without it. Now he wanders the shore, a headless ghost, looking for his head. Or so the legend goes.

The other prime attraction close to Port Rowan is the Backus Heritage Conservation Area (519-586-2201), just north of town on the main road. The 1,240-acre property was originally owned by John Backhouse, who built a mill there in 1788. The mill was one of a handful that escaped destruction by American soldiers during the War of 1812. Historians say that the mill went undetected by the invading army because it sits in a valley. John Backus, a Port Rowan resident and descendent of the original Backhouse, has a different story. "Some people say the American general was a Mason and he spared the mill because John Backhouse was also a Mason, but we'll never know for sure."

The mill, which is the oldest continually-operating grist mill in Ontario, is part of a Heritage Village which also includes a carriage house, ice house, sawmill, barn and blacksmith shop. There is a weaving shop where demonstration are given, and Aunt Erie's Kitchen, where visitors can sample home-made pies and other goodies. A museum in the village contains exhibits about early businesses in the area and about the lost "treasures" of Lake Erie. The unusual schoolhouse on the grounds was built in the 1860s in the shape of an octagon. As close as builders could come to constructing a circle, the octagon was considered a symbol of perfection, theoretically spurring students to pursue the same. Like most of the buildings in the village, the school was moved here from another location. The village is open every day during the summer months, but weekday visitors may find the museum locked, Aunt Erie's Kitchen closed, and the weavers absent. Weekends are a better bet.

The Conservation building, located just inside the park entrance, keeps more regular hours. The attractive center features exhibits about the natural and human history of the Long Point area and nearby Backus Woods.

Backus Woods, which is adjacent to the park, was also part of the original Backhouse property until 1956, when the family sold it to the Big Creek Region Conservation Authority, which now manages it. One of the best remaining examples of Carolinian Forest, Backus Woods is forested with many trees that are unheard of in other parts of Canada. The tempering effect of the lake makes it possible for tulip, sassafras and sweet chestnut trees to thrive, species that are usually found much farther south (thus the term "Carolinian").

The Backus family used the land for orchards and tobacco fields, now overgrown with pine forest, and for logging. Timber from the property was used to build the locks on the Welland Canal. Maple syrup harvested produced by the Backus family was sent yearly to the household of Chaing Kai-Shek until the outbreak of World War II. (Want to know more? As of this writing, John, Tom and George Backus still live in Port Rowan. Tom and John can often be found at the information booth in town. They have many stories of their family and of life as it used to be in the Long Point area.)

Seven-and-a-half miles of hiking trails wind through the woods. There are guided hikes periodically throughout the year. For a schedule of events, contact the conservation area office at the phone number above.

Where to stay:

Bayview Bed & Breakfast
45 Wolven Street
PO Box 9
Port Rowan, Ontario N0E 1M0
519-586-3413

Laura-Jane Charlton and Ron Duncan had only a couple of years to go until retirement from their life-long careers in education. On holiday, they happened to visit the Bayview B & B, owned at the time by Gary and Gloria Silverthorn, who now run a doll and gift shop in Port Dover. The B & B was for sale...and you know the rest of the story. They each took a leave of absence from their jobs and together they embarked on a new adventure. (And not wanting to get too relaxed in their new lifestyle, they decided to open a restaurant as well. See below.) Their modern, air-conditioned home has two guest rooms with shared bath and one suite with private bath that can sleep up to six people. Children are welcome. Laura-Jane serves a full breakfast of bacon and eggs, home made granola and toast.

Where to eat:

The Fish & Chipper
27 Main Street
519-586-3468

Boardwalk over the marsh at Selkirk Provincial Park.

When Laura-Jane and Ron aren't busy taking care of guests at the Bayview B & B, they can be found popping fish into the fryer at the Fish & Chipper, in the heart of downtown Port Rowan. Their specialty is real British-style halibut and "chips" (Americans, read "fries"), but they haven't neglected Lake Erie yellow perch and walleye. For non-fish types there are chicken strips.

For more information contact the Port Rowan Chamber of Commerce, PO Box 357, Port Rowan, Ontario N0E 1M0; 519-586-2762.

NATURAL ATTRACTIONS
Rock Point Provincial Park
In the years following the War of 1812, when Canada was still wary of American attacks, a large naval base was built on the Lake Erie shore near the mouth of the Grand River and in the surrounding area. Soldiers and schooners guarded the shoreline

from what was believed to be a real threat of aggression. It never came, and by 1827 the naval base was in ruins. By 1834, the base was officially closed and the land parceled off. It wasn't until 1957, however, that a portion of it was purchased by the Ontario government and developed into Rock Point Provincial Park.

Rock Point is Ontario's eastern-most provincial park on the lake. Located about midway between Fort Erie and Port Dover, the park has a campground, picnic area, beach, playground and hiking trails. A short trail at the western edge of the park leads to an overlook that affords a nice view of the lake and of Mohawk Island.

Today, the island is an uninhabited breeding ground for water fowl, designated a National Wildlife Area, but it has had a human history. Located in the path of an important navigational route, the island posed a danger for ships on their way to the Welland Canal. In 1846, a lighthouse was constructed as a safeguard, and John Burgess was hired as the first lightkeeper. The manually operated light had to be wound every morning, but one day the mechanism that rotated the light failed. Burgess and his son stayed by the light for the entire night, waving a blanket continually in front of it to simulate the rotation of the beacon so that no ships would be lost on the surrounding reef. In a story with a more tragic ending, lighthouse keeper Richard Foster and his son died in the winter of 1932 while attempting to cross the ice from the island to the mainland.

It's not often that parks are associated with natural gas wells, but there are five of them on the Rock Point property, capable of producing enough fuel to meet the daily needs of 120 households. Three are used to provide hot water and heat in the administration building during the winter, while the other two are on reserve for future needs. Where did this surprising resource come from? The park sits in the middle of an area rich in fossil fuels, remnants of the Devonian period when what is now Lake Erie was a large salt water sea. As the remains of marine organism decayed and were compressed by sediments above, they produced natural gas and petroleum (though there has been no petroleum found within the park boundaries).

The park abounds with fossilized remains of these marine species, which can be viewed in specific areas, particularly a limestone shelf in the southeast corner of the park. A pamphlet, *"Fossils in Rock Point Provincial Park,"* is available at the park office.

Rock Point Provincial Park, PO Box 158, Dunnville, Ontario N1A 2X5; 905-774-6642.

Selkirk Provincial Park

Located about 10 miles east of Port Dover, Selkirk Provincial Park occupies an area first settled by disgruntled Loyalists who left the newly-formed United States shortly after the American Revolution. In the 19th century, Sandusk Creek, part of which is in the park, was the site of a shipbuilding business. The land became a park in 1966.

Although there is a small stone beach, the attraction here is Spring Creek, which flows into the lake. Bordered by marshes, the creek is an excellent place for visitors to canoe or kayak through a rich natural environment where herons and other waterfowl are often spotted. Unfortunately, there is no canoe rental — although there is a launch area — so visitors must have their own boat.

Wheeler's Walk Trail winds about a mile and a half through woods, meadows and across a boardwalk over the marsh, offering an opportunity to explore varied habitats in a short distance. The woods are alive with birds, black squirrels, and the inevitable mosquitoes. Don't venture here in the summer without insect repellent. The trail may be muddy or overgrown in places, so hiking boots aren't a bad idea.

The park has 142 campsites, 60 of them with electrical hookups, in the area bordering the creek. The lakefront and beach is reserved for day use. There is a picnic area and playground overlooking the lake. Selkirk Provincial Park, R.R. 1, Selkirk, Ontario N0A 1P0; 905-776-2600.

Turkey Point Provincial Park

Like much of the lake's northeastern shore, the area around Turkey Point Provincial Park was settled by Loyalists who fled the U. S. after the Revolutionary War. At one time Fort Norfolk stood nearby, poised to protect settlers from American attacks. During the 1800s the town of Normandale, to the east on the lake, was the location of a thriving iron ore foundry. When the supply of bog iron dried up, the town likewise shrank, and today it's a one-blinker — one blink driving by and you've missed it.

The park, named for the wild turkeys found in the area, is really two parks in one, divided by the village of Turkey Point. The park's wide, sandy beach, about a mile and a half long, is one of the nicest along the lake. Just across the street is the village, a beach town complete with ice cream stands, snack shops and an arcade. The bluff that rises sharply above the town marks the border of the other, larger section of the park.

Here visitors will find a 195-site campground, golf course, day-use area and two hiking trails. The short Bluff Lookout Trail loops from the park entrance road out toward the lake to a lookout over the village of Turkey Point and the lake beyond. It is wide and well-marked, part of it paved with gravel, but is lined with poison ivy and inhabited by a multitude of mosquitoes. Points along the trail are marked with numbers that correspond to those on a map/brochure available at the park office, which provides information about the natural history of the area and its many plant and animal species.

The one-mile Fin and Feather Trail, which begins in the northwestern corner of the park, runs out of the park boundary to the Normandale Fish Culture Station, a hatchery, where it meets up with the Rainbow Ridge Trail. This 1.5-mile loop trail winds around a pond which was formerly used as a fish hatchery, through wetlands, marsh and forest, and across a dam before rejoining the Fin and Feather Trail. From there it's another mile back to the park. Map trails are available at the park office.

Turkey Point Provincial Park, PO Box 5, Turkey Point, Ontario

N0E 1T0; 519-426-3239.

Long Point Provincial Park

The peninsula at Long Point is the longest and wildest on Lake Erie. Designated a World Biosphere Reserve by the United Nations, Long Point provides habitats for a variety of birds, reptiles, amphibians and plants. Most of the point is occupied by the Long Point National Wildlife Area and the Long Point Company, a private concern that has done much to preserve the peninsula. Unfortunately for the visitor, both of these properties are off-limits, except for a beach in the wildlife area that is accessible only by boat.

What remains is the Big Creek National Wildlife Area at the base of the peninsula, bordered by an overdeveloped section of cottages and RV parks, and the relatively small parcel of land that makes up Long Point Provincial Park.

Long Point can be disappointing for those who expect miles of pristine shoreline. There're there; you just can't walk on them. Certainly, for the visitor, Long Point can't begin to compare with Point Pelee National Park, farther to the west.

Most of the park is devoted to campsites — 261 of them, although there is a day use area with a beautiful golden sand beach. Perhaps the most interesting way to spend a day at Long Point is to explore the water and marshy areas of Long Point Bay, abundant with bass, pike, walleye, perch, trout and salmon. Although there are no boat rentals available at the park, nearby marinas do rent boats, and there's a launch ramp on the bay side of the park. Caution should be exercised, however, because of the bay's shallow nature and its uncanny ability to churn up into an angry demon at the slightest provocation. Park officials warn visitors not to attempt to round the tip of the point into the open lake. The fact that more ships per square foot have been lost in this little puddle of water than in any where else in the world is a sobering reminder of its treacherous personality.

Deer ticks carrying Lyme disease have been found at Long Point

The overlook at Rock Point Provincial Park.

(as well as many other parks along the lake — especially Presque Isle State Park in Pennsylvania), so precautions are necessary. When in areas of thick vegetation wear long sleeves and long pants, with the cuffs tucked into your socks. Use an insect repellent and check yourself and your clothing for ticks afterwards.

Long Point Provincial Park, PO Box 99, Port Rowan Ontario N0E 1M0; 519-586-2133.

DIVERSIONS
Niagara Falls

Just about a 20-minute drive along the Niagara Parkway from Fort Erie is one of the most memorable sights on the North American continent. More than six million cubic feet of water plummets over Niagara Falls every minute. While it's a spectacle from either the American or Canadian side, Canada has the

States beat hands down for the beauty of the surrounding area. Canada has done an admirable job of keeping the falls immaculately groomed and attractive, with its flower gardens and wide expanse of lawns. Visitors can simply walk and enjoy the scenery or they can do the "falls" things — take the Maid of the Mist boat tour, walk behind a section of the falls, hover over it in a cable car, or walk beside the gorge created by the river. A new addition to the falls area is the Niagara Parks Butterfly Conservatory, a 11,000-square-foot indoor tropical rain forest populated with thousands of exotic butterflies. They flutter at arm's length, light on your shoulders, and feed on the flowers that grow abundantly in the warm, moist habitat. It's worth going to Niagara Falls just for a visit to this unique and beautiful place. For more information contact the Niagara Parks Commission at PO Box 150, Niagara Falls, Ontario L2E 6T2; 905-356-2241.

Niagara River

While the big attraction on the Niagara River is the falls, the river itself is worth more than a look. This beautiful waterway winds past manicured residential areas with road side parks, alongside a 35-mile recreation trail that runs from Fort Erie to Niagara-on-the-Lake. Its smooth, paved surface makes it perfect for walking, cycling and in-line skating.

For some, it's what's in the river that is interesting. During Prohibition, Canadian rum runners had a field day on the Niagara, the narrowest passage from Canada to the U.S. Midnight runs were the usual method, though a surprise visit by U.S. officials prompted many a smuggler to dump his load into the river. Scuba divers are still finding them today, and miraculously, occasionally a full bottle is still found. In addition, the bottom of the clear, shallow river (about 20-50 feet) is littered with antique china and other artifacts. For more information contact Great Niagara Dive Charters, 1999 Jewson Road, Fort Erie, Ontario L2A 5M4; 905-871-9303.

WHAT'S A CONSERVATION AREA?

To Americans, "conservation area" might mean something akin to a preserve. The term has an entirely different meaning in Canada, though, where a conservation area is usually a place set aside for recreational purposes, primarily camping, picnicking and swimming. Three Conservation Areas on the eastern Ontario shore offer these activities. There are fees for both day-use and camping. They vary considerably in degree of attractiveness, the primary detractor being the often tightly squeezed platoon of camper vehicles and RVs, many of which are parked for the season. But just in case, here they are:

Long Beach Conservation Area
(905-899-3462), south of Wainfleet, has a long sandy beach and 240 camping sites. It is one of the more attractive conservation areas.

Haldiman Conservation Area
(905-776-2700), southwest of Selkirk, is small, crowded with seasonal camper vehicles (as many as 124 of them) and in the shadows of the Nanticoke power plant towers. There are 40 sites for transient campers.

Norfolk Conservation Area
(519-428-1460), just west of Port Ryerse, has 170 transient sites.

Welland Canal

The 26-mile Welland Canal with its eight locks joins Lake Ontario to Lake Erie, by-passing the 326-foot drop at Niagara Falls. Ships as long as 730 feet make the 12-hour transit at the rate of about 3,000 a year. While one of the best places for viewing the canal is at Lock 8 in Port Colborne, Lock 3 in St. Catharines also has a viewing platform as well as an interpretive center and gift shop. The Welland Recreational Waterway, a section of the old canal no longer used for shipping, now serves as a location for boating, water-skiing and picnicking. Adjacent to it is Merritt Island, a great place for hiking, biking, picnicking and cross-country skiing in the winter. For those who want to explore the canal by foot or bicycle, the 28-mile Merritt Trail is ideal. The well-marked gravel trail winds along the canal from Port Colborne to St. Catharines, many parts of which are inaccessible by car. For more information on the canal contact the Region Niagara Tourist Council, Box 1042, Thorold, Ontario L2V 4T7; phone 416-685-3626.

Selkirk

Just north of the small town of Selkirk is Cottonwood Mansion (905-776-2538), built in 1865 by William Holmes, Jr., from Ontario. When his wife Mary died, he remarried and at the age of 61 fathered a girl, Lillian. She must have been a favorite because William left the entire 100-acre property and house to her in his will. His wife got life-time use of their bedroom. When Lillian married, her widower husband and family moved to Cottonwood and they began a new family. Lillian sold the place in 1911 and it fell into ruin. Restoration began in 1988 when the house was leased and later sold to a non-profit corporation. Incredibly, Lillian's first-born child, Helen, was located at the age of 93 in Oregon. She was able to provide much information about the house and its inhabitants. Although she passed away before she could return to visit Cottonwood, many of her personal items were send there at her request. The magnificent 15-room, 6,000 square-foot home is open to visitors 10 a.m. - 4 p.m. Tuesday through Saturday; 1 - 4 p.m. Sundays. It is closed on Mondays.

Just west of Selkirk on Route 3 is the Wilson MacDonald Memorial School Museum (905-776-3319), one of only a handful of local one-room school houses that remain in its original form (many have been turned into private residences). Built in 1867, it was in continuous use until 1965. In 1967, it was turned into a museum and named in honor of Wilson Pugsley MacDonald, a local poet who achieved acclaim and who died that same year.

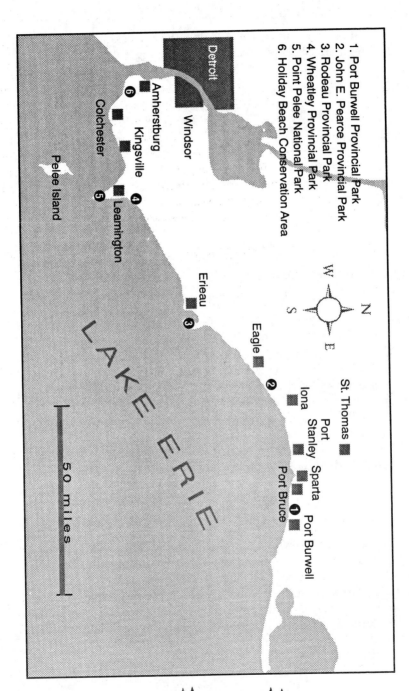

1. Port Burwell Provincial Park
2. John E. Pearce Provincial Park
3. Rodeau Provincial Park
4. Wheatley Provincial Park
5. Point Pelee National Park
6. Holiday Beach Conservation Area

Detroit

Windsor

Amherstburg

Colchester

Kingsville

Pelee Island

Learnington

Erieau

LAKE ERIE

Eagle

St. Thomas

Iona

Port Stanley

Sparta

Port Bruce

Port Burwell

50 miles

Chapter Six

Western Ontario
In the Footsteps of Colonel Talbot

The western lake shore plunges even deeper into Ontario's agricultural heartland. Cherry orchards, strawberry fields and acres of tobacco pave the way nearly into Windsor. Roadside produce stands and "pick your own" farms abound. This is Canada's *"Banana Belt,"* so named because the modifying effect of the lake allows crops to grow here in an abundance unseen anywhere else in the country. With the exception of Pelee Island, this strip of lake shore is the southernmost occupied land in Canada. Folks from farther north call visiting this area "going south."

The area also has historical significance that sets it aside from other places. Towns with names like Port Talbot and Talbotville, streets called Talbot Road East Branch and Talbot Road North Branch, and even a Talbot River, are constant reminders that the route along the lake follows what is known as the Talbot Trail. Named for Colonel Thomas Talbot, the trail, which is marked by signs along the road, retraces the original road built by Talbot in 1809 after he was charged with the task of developing the area. Canada was casting nervous glances across the lake at the time, afraid that its sparsely populated land would fall victim to American expansion.

Talbot, himself a baron, was anything but egalitarian in choosing settlers for the land under his domain. Tyrannical and despotic, he wanted absolute control of who lived on Lake Erie's north shore, and where. Never actively recruiting settlers, he was content to dole out parcels as he saw fit to those who appeared at his doorstep with the determination to set down roots. There were those he called "land pirates," who for one reason or another didn't meet the colonel's criteria, and whom he turned away without compunction. After one disgruntled rejectee threw Talbot to the ground, he devised a sliding window that separated him from his prospective tenants. If they didn't meet his favor, he slammed the window and called out the dogs.

Those who did gain Talbot's approval were overwhelmingly Irish and Scottish. They settled and began farming, founding such towns as Tyrconnell, Port Glasgow and Iona. Stop at one of the old cemeteries by the side of the road and you'll find that many inscriptions end with the words "Native of Scotland."

Towns on this end of the lake are more scattered and smaller than those of Canada's eastern shore, with even more land given over to farming. Even Leamington, the largest of these, owes its prosperity to the land — its largest employer is the Heinz Company, which processes the fruit of the *"Tomato Capital of Canada."* Despite its rural nature, Ontario's western shore holds some of the lake's best and little-known treats.

The town of Port Stanley offers everything a good lake town should — great shopping, excellent restaurants and places to stay, sandy beaches and picturesque scenery. Port Burwell, at the mouth of Big Otter Creek, has one of the oldest and most attractive lighthouses on the lake. And Point Pelee National Park, near Leamington, is the foremost natural attraction on the lake — a glimpse, preserved in time, of what much of the lake shore must have looked like nearly 200 years ago when Colonel Talbot first set his eyes on the place he called "paradise."

PLACES

Port Burwell

Twelve miles west of Long Point, Lakeshore Road passes by

The dunes at Sand Hill Park.

Sand Hill Park (519-586-3891), location of the highest dunes on Lake Erie. Towering 450 feet above the shoreline, these dunes were probably used as lookout points by the Neutral Indians who inhabited the area before the arrival of Europeans. In 1854, John Alton bought the property, which was then a farm. In 1870, the United States Lake Survey built an observatory at the top of the dunes. Similar ones were built at Long Point and across the lake in Pennsylvania, and with data received from all three points, accurate surveying of the lake was able to take place. In the 1890s, Alton began charging 10 cents to those who came to see the dunes, and a commercial operation was born. Today, the dunes, which are owned by John Alton's descendants, are part of a camping and picnicking facility open to the public May 1 to Thanksgiving.

Another eight miles down the road is Port Burwell, home of the Otter Valley Optimist Club and Lake Erie's only annual bathtub race. Though quiet and unassuming, Port Burwell has its share of character.

On August 18, 1984, Ed Matthews popped a 1930 Johnson Sea Horse outdoor motor on the back of a bathtub, hopped in and motored his makeshift vessel from Port Burwell across the lake to Erie, Pennsylvania. His motive was to raise money for the Ronald McDonald House in London, Ontario, and to promote Port Burwell. Little did he know he was establishing a tradition. Every summer a fleet of porcelain-lined dinghies hit the water for the Lake Erie Bathtub Race, giving literal meaning to the word "tub" when used to describe a less-than-elegant means of water transportation.

But long before Matthews' stunt, Port Burwell was known for something else. The Port Burwell Lighthouse, Canada's oldest wooden lighthouse, stands close to where Big Otter Creek flows into Lake Erie. Built in 1840, the lighthouse served as a ships' beacon until its closing in 1963. It had been manned by the Sutherland family of Port Burwell for over a century. The lighthouse underwent extensive renovation in 1986 and today is the town's major tourist attraction. While the lower part serves as the tourist office, visitors can climb the wooden staircase to the top for a panoramic view of the town and the harbor area. It is open daily during July and August, other times by appointment (519-874-4204 or 519-874-4343).

Although it's quiet today, the harbor was once the site of bustling activity. The town, named after Col. Mahlon Burwell, was part of a parcel of land given to Burwell by Talbot as a reward for his services as land surveyor. By 1836 there were 200 inhabitants. A flourishing shipbuilding industry soon developed, using the hardwood that was floated down Big Otter Creek from the lumberyards up north. Seventy-one sailing ships were built at Port Burwell during the lake's heyday of shipbuilding in the 19th century. The shipping of lumber and commercial fishing also played important roles in the town's development.

Though not built at Port Burwell, the schooner Nimrod has inadvertently become a part of the town's history. The 184-foot vessel sank near Port Bruce in 1874, just a year after it had been built in Toledo, Ohio. Caught in a early morning fog, the ship's crew had only 15 seconds to change course once they spotted the schooner Michigan directly in their path. The inevitable occurred, and the Nimrod went down in 70 feet of water. The captain of the Michigan, not realizing the extent of the damage, had sailed on into the fog. The Nimrod went undiscovered for over a hundred years until it was found by a fisherman whose gill net became caught on its wreckage. The ship remains in its final resting spot, but the anchor sits next to Port Burwell's lighthouse. Brought to the surface by marine archeologist Mick Verbrugge and Port Burwell resident Tony Lama in 1979, the 3,000-pound anchor was donated to the village.

The ship's steering wheel can be seen at the Port Burwell Marine Museum (519-874-4204 or 519-874-4343) across the street from the lighthouse. Another ship disaster chronicled at the museum is the sinking of the Ashtabula, a 350-foot rail car ferry that operated between Port Burwell and Ashtabula, Ohio. The last of the rail car ferries on the Great Lakes, the Ashtabula sank in Ashtabula Harbor after a collision in 1958. The port holes are on display at the museum, as well as a large model of the ship. Other displays concern early life in Port Burwell and include household appliances like butter churns and manual washing machines. There's a reconstructed shoemaker's shop and Chalk's Drugstore that operated in the town from the 1930s to the1950s. Among a large collection of pier lights and lenses is the original light and lens from the old lighthouse on Long Point, which is today a private residence. Like the Port Burwell lighthouse, the museum is open daily in July and August, and other times by appointment.

It's a worthwhile trip to visit the Edison Museum (519-874-4999 or 874-4225) in Vienna, just three miles north of town. Though Thomas Alva Edison was born in Milan, Ohio, his family had earlier lived in Vienna. Forced to flee Canada because of his involvement with a rebel uprising, Thomas's father Samuel settled in Milan in 1837. His wife Nancy joined him two years later, and Thomas was born in 1847. The rest of the family had remained behind, and Thomas visited at regular intervals during his childhood. The museum, which is located on the grounds once owned by the Edison family, contains furniture and other artifacts that were donated by Thomas's cousin, Nora Edison Coomb. Many of Thomas Edison's ancestors are buried in the

Edison Pioneer Cemetery, on King Street just outside the village. West of Port Burwell, the road runs through tiny Port Bruce, with its Dairy and Heritage Museum (519-773-8625), open by appointment only. The primary attraction in the town is Port Bruce Provincial Park, a long, sandy beach for day-use only.

Where to eat:

Mamma's Restaurant
43 Robinson St.
519-874-4133

Mamma's serves good homemade food on a pleasant deck overlooking Big Otter Creek. Burgers, sandwiches, fish and chips, pizza, lasagna, chicken and steak are available.

Craigers Cove
Robinson Street
519-874-1117

Just down the street is Craigers, also overlooking Big Otter Creek. The specialty here is fresh lake perch and walleye (pickerel, if you're Canadian). They've gathered such a following over the years that faithful customers drive from miles around to enjoy the food and pleasant view. Craigers does not accept credit cards.

For more information contact the town of Port Burwell at Box 10, Port Burwell, Ontario N0J 1T0; 519-874-4343.

Port Stanley

Nestled in a valley at the mouth of Kettle Creek, Port Stanley vies with Vermilion, Ohio, for the distinction of being the most attractive town on the lake. In fact, it comes pretty close to perfection. There's something here for everyone — for the grown-ups there are sophisticated restaurants, excellent accommodations, interesting boutiques and antiques shops, and a thriving summer theater; for kids there are sandy beaches, miniature golf, ice cream shops, paddle boats and souvenir shops.

Kettle Creek, Port Stanley.

Explorers Dollier and Galinee found their way here in the 1600s. Others passed through after making the portage across Long Point on their way to settlements along the Thames River farther west. In 1832, a ferry service between Buffalo and Port Stanley was established. Throughout the years of settlement Port Stanley's protected harbor was a destination for many American and British ships that came to service the larger inland towns of St. Thomas and London. But it wasn't until the early 1900s that Port Stanley hit her heyday. It was then that the town became the most popular tourist attraction on the lake. Its popularity extended into later years, when the casinos and clubs attracted visitors who came to hear Guy Lombardo and others of the Big Band era.

It's still a holiday town, but on a less grand scale. Several festivals and special events draw visitors throughout the year. There's a Fish Fest in May and a Canada Day celebration in July. August brings C.A.L.I.P.S.O., or *"Come and Live In Port Stanley Ontario,"* a weekend of fun that includes a land parade, boat parade, fireworks, a foot race and even a bed race. In December,

Port Stanley Terminal Rail.

there are the Dickens Days, when the town puts on a Victorian air complete with period costumes, horse and buggy rides, a twilight parade and a Santa train ride. The renowned Port Stanley Festival Theatre (519-782-4353), in the heart of the village, produces plays each summer, June through August.

Train buffs will enjoy the Port Stanley Terminal Rail (519-782-3730). Visitors can ride open or closed coaches pulled by a diesel locomotive from the train station in town to one of three destinations along its route. The tracks follow the old London and Port Stanley Railway that began operations in 1856, carrying tourists to and from Port Stanley and hauling Pennsylvania coal inland. The train chugs through the scenic Kettle Creek valley, past woods, fields and trackside gardens. The first stop is the Union Station, built in 1923. The second is a picnic area at the site of a former station, where a rail snow plow, caboose, tank car and box car are on display. Those who want to ride the entire route will go to St. Thomas, where the locomotive is moved to the other end of the train and the route is reversed. The train runs all year, daily during July and August, less frequently the rest of the year.

Port Stanley is blessed with some of the nicest beaches on the north shore. Little Beach, on the east side of Kettle Creek, is the quietest and most apt to attract families with small children. The Main Beach connects directly with the Pierside Beach on the west side of the creek. Groomed daily, this wide expanse of sandy beach is close to snack bars, restaurants and miniature golf.

Hawk Cliff, just east of town, is an excellent place to view raptors, especially during the fall migration. Broad-winged hawks, falcons, harriers, osprey and eagles all congregate here, as do crowds of eager observers. Large groups of monarch butterflies can also be seen in the fall when they pause here before crossing the lake to make the long trip to their winter home, some 2,000 miles south in Mexico. For more information contact the Hawk Cliff Foundation at PO Box 11, Port Stanley, Ontario N5L 1J4.

The Elgin Hiking Trail winds along for 27 kilometers through valleys and woods along Kettle Creek and Dodds Creek between Port Stanley and St. Thomas. There are numerous side trails and links to the Thames Valley Trail and the Bruce Trail. For more information and a free map contact the Elgin Hiking Trail Club, c/o Kettle Creek Conservation Authority, R.R. 8, St. Thomas, Ontario N5P 3T3 or call 519-633-3064.

In the rural areas outside Port Stanley, farm markets abound. One of the best of these is Empire Valley Farm Market near Wallacetown. Owners Dave and Joy Westelaken grow peppers, tomatoes, sweet corn, cucumbers and some of the best strawberries around. They also sell home-canned treats, like "Dad's Best" pickles and salsa.

Where to stay:

Kettle Creek Inn
216 Joseph Street
Port Stanley, Ontario N5L 1C4
519-782-3388

It's not easy to describe the Kettle Creek Inn. "Country elegance" comes close. The original inn was built in 1849, and though it has been completely renovated it still maintains its charm. Two additional buildings were built in 1990 to house suites and a conference facility. The three buildings are arranged around a center courtyard and patio where dining is available. There are 10 guest rooms with private baths and five luxury suites. Each room or suite is unique. The suites have gas fireplaces, whirlpools and private balconies; one has a cathedral ceiling. Many of the rooms are named after area artists whose work decorate the walls. All have telephone, cable TV, coffee maker and a radio. A complimentary breakfast that includes scones, muffins and croissants baked on the premises is served in the dining room or on the patio. There is an old-fashioned pub on the main floor. While the Kettle Creek Inn may be one of the pricier options on the Canadian shore, it is quite reasonable for the accommodations offered, and actually less expensive than a typical room in a chain motel in the resort area around Ohio's Cedar Point.

Christerville Station B & B
547 Edith Cavelle
Port Stanley, Ontario N5L 1G8
519-782-3123

This is the place for beach lovers. Set in a quiet neighborhood on a private beach just west of town, Christerville Station is more like an apartment than a B & B. It has one air-conditioned suite that includes a living room with fireplace, kitchen, bath and two bedrooms. If only one bedroom is needed, the second one is closed off and the rate is lower. Hosts Bob and Sandy Earle provide a continental breakfast which they bring to the suite. You could hardly ask for a more private place.

The Home Place Bed & Breakfast
297 Bridge Street
Port Stanley, Ontario N5L 1G8
519-782-3846

Host Mary Lynn Jaques, who also owns the boutique downstairs, has done a wonderful job of renovating and decorating this charming B & B in downtown Port Stanley. There are five rooms, including a suite that sleeps four, and two shared baths in the country-Victorian style house. An indoor lap pool and whirlpool occupy the lower level. Mary Lynn provides a full breakfast and will also make up picnic baskets and cook dinner upon request. The B & B is open year-round; from October through May, Mary Lynn hosts Murder Mystery weekends.

Where to eat:

Kettle Creek Inn
216 Joseph Street
519-782-3388

Like the inn where it's located, this restaurant is quietly elegant. Though the menu changes periodically, diners are likely to find appetizers such as chicken and beef satay, arugula and spinach salad, or scallop and shrimp terrine. Dinner entrees may include special preparations of Lake Erie walleye, blackened New York Strip steak or shrimp Pad Thai. Guests may dine in the somewhat formal dining room or, in the summer months, outside on the casual patio.

San Saba
205 Main Street
519-782-5168

This intimate, charming restaurant serves small portions of tapas-style food such as coconut shrimp, samosas, chicken satay, and blackened catfish salad. For those who want a traditional meal, there are a few selections of full dinners available. The restaurant, which is in an old home, has both indoor and outdoor dining.

For more information contact the St. Thomas-Elgin Tourist Association, PO Box 22042, St. Thomas, Ontario; 519-631-8188.

Leamington

Visitors searching for the information booth need only look for the giant tomato, located off Talbot Street on the north end of town. Leamington, the Tomato Capital of Ontario, is home of the

Leamington's visitors information booth.

world's largest tomato, and proud of it. The roads leading into the town are lined with tomato stands, which raises the question of who buys them, since everyone seems to grow them. The H.J. Heinz Company, the town's largest employer, dominates the downtown area. There's an annual Tomato Festival the third week in August each year. There's no getting away from tomatoes in Leamington, except maybe to sample the cucumbers, asparagus, beans, corn, onions, melons, peaches, grapes or strawberries that are also grown in abundance here.

Leamington is the southernmost town in mainland Canada, and much is made of this fact. *"Southern Latitude, Friendly Attitude"* is a slogan often seen. The town has one of the highest percentages of senior citizens in Canada, drawn to the mild climate like American seniors are lured to Florida.

For visitors it's not Leamington itself that's the attraction — it's what is close by. The biggest draw, especially during the spring bird migration, is Point Pelee National Park, the only national park — Canadian or American — on Lake Erie. Leamington is

FOLLOWING THE WINE ROUTE

All along Route 18 west of Leamington are signs depicting clusters of grapes. These mark the Wine Route through Ontario's Lake Erie Shore wine region. Designated as one of three distinct wine-producing regions in Ontario (the other two are Pelee Island and the Niagara Peninsula on Lake Ontario), the north shore enjoys a sunny climate and long growing seasons, making it ideal for grape-growing. Local producers are quick to point out to skeptics that this area lies at approximately the same latitude as the famous wine-producing regions of Chianti, Rioja, Provence and Oregon. Following the Wine Route to the following four wineries makes a pleasant afternoon excursion. Tours are usually at specific times or must be pre-arranged, so call for details beforehand.

Pelee Island Winery (519-733-6551 or 1-800-597-3533) in Kingsville produces wines from grapes grown on nearby Pelee Island. Winemaker Walter Schmoranz does a fine job, resulting in excellent wines such as Pinot Noir, Chardonnay and Gewurztraminer. The winery offers tours and tastings seven days a week year round. Call for tour times. From May to October, the Wine Pavilion on Pelee Island has tours and barbecue lunches.

Farther west on Route 18 in Harrow is Colio Estate Wines (519-738-2241), one of the largest of the Ontario wineries, founded in 1981. With the expertise of winemaker Carlo Negri, Colio has produced award-winning Vidal Icewine, Pinot Gris, Riesling Traminer and Cabernet Franc. Tours and tastings are offered Monday through Saturday throughout the year. The winery extends its hours to include Sundays, May to October. Call for a tour schedule.

Just north of Harrow is the Le Blanc Estate Winery (519-738-9228). The smallest and newest of the area's wineries, Le Blanc has only 25 acres of vines, but has nonetheless produced award-winning wines.

The D'Angelo Estate Winery (519-736-7959) is located on Concession 5 east of Amherstburg. Winemaker and owner Sal D'Angelo has won awards for his Cabernet-Merlot, Marechal Foch and Chardonnay. Although the on-site retail store is open year-round, tours and tastings are by appointment only. D'Angelo also sells grape juice and wine-making supplies to amateur winemakers.

Pelee Island Winery, Colio Estate Wines and D'Angelo Estate Winery are recognized by the Vintners Quality Alliance (VQA) as adhering to a strict set of standards for producing fine wines.

also the departure point for Pelee Island, an hour-and-a-half ferry ride south.

There is little in the way of historical interest in Leamington — no museums or similar attractions. The town is not particularly attractive, though its park and marina are. Seacliff Park, just west of the downtown business district, has a grassy, shaded picnic area on a hill overlooking the lake. There are grills, a playground and a sprinkle pool for small children. The park slopes down to the water, ending at a sandy beach with rest rooms and a concession stand.

Adjacent to the park is the public dock, where the Pelee Island ferries board. Two ferries presently operate — the large, new M.V. Jiimaan, which looks much like a floating billboard; and the smaller, dependable Pelee Islander. From March until early December, it's possible to get to the island by ferry, though from late summer on, the ferries depart from Kingsville, farther west. During late spring and summer, the ferry stops at Pelee Island and then sails on for Sandusky, Ohio, another hour-and-forty-five minutes south. Cars can be taken on the ferries, but reservations fill quickly, so be sure to plan ahead. Passengers without vehicles do not need reservations. Day-trips from Leamington are quite popular, and the ferry is often crowded in the summer months with tourists heading for the Pelee Island Wine Pavilion, where they will have a tour and tasting followed by a barbecue lunch.

Leamington Municipal Marina (519-326-0834), on Robson Road east of the dock, has new and attractive facilities including a children's play area, picnic area with gas barbecue, volleyball court, snack and souvenir concessions and bike rentals. There is a brick promenade connecting the marina with the municipal dock.

About five miles southeast of Leamington is Point Pelee National Park, home of rare plants, stopover for migrating birds and one of Canada's few Carolinian forests. There are miles of clean, sandy beaches, bike paths, hiking trails and a boardwalk over an extensive marsh. For more information see the "*Natural Attractions*" section later in this chapter.

Those heading to Point Pelee National Park may wish to stop first at Pelee Wings Nature Store (519-326-5193), located on Point Pelee Drive just before the entrance to the park. The store specializes in birding paraphernalia, including binoculars and telescopes as well as local and regional bird guides. There is also a large selection of nature oriented gifts. Pelee Wings rents kayaks, a great way to explore the park's marsh areas. The store is closed January 1 to April 15.

Where to stay:

Home Suite Home Bed and Breakfast
115 Erie Street
Leamington, Ontario N8H 3B5
519-326-7169

In the heart of Leamington a few blocks from the ferry dock, Home Suite Home is a turn-of-the-century home, which is decorated in Victorian style. Rooms with private bath or shared bath are available. There's a large in-ground pool that makes a welcome diversion on a hot afternoon. Owners Harry and Aggie Tiessen serve a full country breakfast that includes items like home-made peach crepes. Aggie is the coordinator of the Point

Petting a baby quail at Jack Miner Bird Sanctuary.

Pelee Bed & Breakfast Reservation Service, which maintains a listing of 30 area B & Bs.

Park Gate Bed and Breakfast Beachfront
866 Point Pelee Drive
R.R. #1, Leamington, Ontario N8H 3V4
519-326-3732

Just a mile from the park's gates (hence the name), this is a great place for people whose primary interest is visiting the park or who prefer a quiet location away from the town. Hosts Theresa and Clair Chase have a casual, air-conditioned B & B with a deck right on the lake. Guests can swim or paddle away in canoes provided by the Chases when the water is calm. There are two guest rooms with TV on the second floor; one has a king-size bed with a private balcony and the other has one double and one twin bed. There are one and a half baths on the lower level. Breakfast is geared to your wants — homemade toast and jam with seasonal fresh fruit or the works, including bacon, eggs and pancakes for birders with hearty appetites.

An albino Rock dove, one of many injured birds cared for at Jack Miner Bird Sanctuary.

Where to eat:

Thirteen Russell Steak House
13 Russell Street
519-325-8401

This is the place to go if you want elegant dining in Leamington. Located on a quiet side street, Thirteen Russell was originally a house built by Leamington resident Adolphus Brown at the turn of the century. It's reported that the house was the first in the town to have indoor plumbing. Old house aficionados will enjoy the ornate wood work and stained glass windows. Everyone will enjoy the ambiance and excellent food. The specialty is steak, but there is chicken, shrimp, pasta, and salmon as well as other entrees and daily specials.

Leamington Dock Restaurant
Foot of Erie Street
519-326-2697

With an appearance akin to an overgrown tin shack, Leamington Dock is none too inviting from the outside. However, it's not unusual for a long line to form at the door, testament that food, not appearance, reigns. Fried lake perch and walleye cooked in many preparations are the specialties. Service is friendly if not always speedy, but this is a great place to spend time people-watching out the window at the continuous stream of folks driving around the dock.

For more information contact the Leamington District Chamber of Commerce PO Box 321, Leamington, Ontario N8H 3W3; 519-326-2721.

Kingsville and Vicinity

Scattered along the shore between Leamington and Amherstburg are several attractions worth a stop. Kingsville, the largest town in this area, is the best bet for accommodations and dining.

Colasanti's Tropical Gardens (519-326-3287), in Ruthven between Leamington and Kingsville, resembles a cross between a plant nursery, a zoo and an amusement park. Their greenhouses contain 3.5-acres of tropical plants and cacti, proof of Essex County's mild climate and wealth of sunshine. But that's not all. Visitors will also find a petting zoo, restaurant, tropical birds, kiddie rides and indoor mini-golf. Though it's not as attractive or well maintained as Swain's (see *Diversions*) farther east in Eagle, it's worth a stop. And the kids will love it.

On a back road north of Kingsville is one of the most visited sites in this part of Canada. It's not unusual to encounter people speaking Spanish, Japanese or French — or any of a dozen other languages. What draws people here is the Jack Miner Bird Sanctuary (519-733-4034).

Jack Miner was born near Cleveland, Ohio, in 1865. Son of a brick maker, Miner was 13 when he and his family moved to the still wild area around Kingsville. Miner grew up to become an avid hunter, guiding expeditions into northern Quebec and

Ontario. But in 1903 he had a realization that changed the course of his life. While hunting geese, he became alarmed by their cries of distress when they realized the danger he presented. Yet those same geese flew unconcerned over the heads of two men working the land nearby. Somehow they recognized enemies. If so, they might recognize friends. He set out to become one.

In 1904, he bought seven geese whose wings had been clipped and brought them to his farm to live. He hoped that their presence would entice others to come. He convinced neighbors not to shoot geese flying overhead. In return he promised that if the migrating geese rested at his farm they would be allowed to hunt a limited number. Years went by and no geese stopped. People began to make fun of Miner, laughing at him and greeting him with a derisive "Honk!"

Then, in the spring of 1908, 11 geese settled at his pond. As he had promised, he allowed his neighbors to shoot five. The next spring he waited, wondering if the geese would return. Thirty-two geese came that spring. In 1910, 400 arrived. In 1911, they came in a swarm that darkened the skies over Miner's farm, as many as 25,000 thick. That was the beginning of the Jack Miner Bird Sanctuary, and the beginning of new work for Miner.

He gave his life over to the sanctuary, growing corn to feed the multitudes of birds that sought refuge on his land and traveling to give lectures about bird life and his work. He planted trees as windbreaks and enlarged his pond to a two-acre lake. He and his son established a hospital for injured birds, who seemed to find their way to the Miner farm as readily as the healthy ones.

Miner began to wonder about the routes ducks and geese followed on their migratory journeys every year. One day he attached a band to a duck's leg with his name and address on it. The following year he received word from a hunter in South Carolina who had shot the duck. That initiated a whole new focus for Miner. He would find out as much as he could about the flyways birds had used for millennia. By the time of his death in 1944, Miner had tagged and tracked more than 50,000 ducks and 31,000 geese, each one bearing his name and a verse from the Bible. He kept a chart of his findings, a map dotted with red to mark the places his birds were found. No one had ever thought to do such a thing before.

Henry Ford and Ty Cobb came to visit, and both supported his work financially. When Miner turned 79, Princess Juliana of the Netherlands sent her congratulations and King George VI conferred upon him the Order of the British Empire. At the time of his death, Miner was a famous and an honored man. In 1947, Canada declared the week of his birthday, April 10, as National Wildlife Week.

The sanctuary lives on. The geese still come in numbers that defy imagination and injured birds are still nursed back to health. In accordance with Jack Miner's will, no admission is charged, and the sanctuary is closed on Sundays. Nothing is sold on the grounds — no souvenirs, no snacks, no drinks. For as Jack Miner declared, *"Let there be one place on earth where no money changes hands."*

The sanctuary is administered by the Jack Miner Migratory Bird Foundation, a private foundation. It is open Monday through Saturday year-round from 8 a.m. to sundown. The small museum on the grounds is open 9 a.m. to 5 p.m. The best times to view migrating birds are the last two weeks of October, all of November, the last two weeks of March and the first week of April.

On the shore road between Kingsville and Colchester is the John Park Homestead and Conservation Area (519-738-2029). Unlike most Conservation Areas, which serve as campgrounds and day-use recreation facilities, John Park is a historical site similar to the Backus Conservation Center in Port Rowan. Consisting of a house and outbuildings, it served as home to John R. Park and his two brothers, Thomas and Theodore, in the early 1820s. After Thomas and Theodore moved to Amherstburg to manage the shipping and trading business the brothers had built up, John stayed behind and ran the 114-acre farm, sawmill and store on the property. He later married Amelia Gamble and over the years they had six children whom they raised on the farm. When John retired to Amherstburg, Francis Fox bought the house and it remained in his family for the next hundred years. It is now administered by Essex Region Conservation.

The house is in amazingly good condition, with the original woodwork made from local trees, including tulip wood, which is rare in Canada. The house is furnished as it might have been during the Park's residence, and there are period artifacts scattered throughout. Also on the property are a blacksmith shop, an outhouse, a smoke house, ice house, barn and sawmill. One of the park's most unique aspects is that, with the exception of the sawmill, these are the original buildings in their original locations. (At other similar facilities the historic buildings have been moved from other areas to the site). Its striking location just a few feet from the lake makes the house and property a particularly pleasant place to visit. Visitors can view a video about the park at the visitors' center, followed by a guided tour by volunteers in period costumes. There's a picnic area nearby.

If you've always wondered what's beneath Lake Erie's waters, but you're not a scuba diver, Wreck Exploration Tours (519-326-1566 or 1-800-667-0118) will give you the chance. The tour begins at Colchester harbor where visitors board a large boat equipped with a TV monitor. Owner Mike Mullen gives an overview of the lake's nautical history, including the shipping and shipbuilding industries and their inevitable by-product, shipwrecks. While anchored over the site of a nineteenth century wooden schooner, divers descend with a video camera to transmit pictures back to the boat. It's a unique opportunity for an underwater view of the lake that holds the most shipwrecks per square mile of any body of fresh water in the world.

Where to stay:

Kingswood Inn Bed & Breakfast
101 Mill Street West
Kingsville, ON N9Y 1W4
519-733-3248

This lovely home was built by Kingsville's founder, Col. James S. King, in 1859. The unusual octagonal-shaped building is located in a quiet residential area on a three-and-a-half-acre grassy lot. There are five guest rooms, each with air-conditioning and private bath. The home is richly furnished with antiques and decorated with fine art. Hosts Jay and Helen Koop and their daughter and son-in-law, Barb and Bob, serve a full buffet breakfast. There is a large in-ground swimming pool and a two-person whirlpool. The inn is open year-round, but limited to weekends during January and the first half of February. This is among the most luxurious of the B & Bs on the Canadian shore. As can be expected, it is pricier than most.

Where to eat:

The Vintage Goose
24 Main Street West
519-733-6900

This cozy, elegant restaurant in downtown Kingsville is owned by the Loop family, who also own and run the Tin Goose Inn and Gooseberry's Island Cuisine on Pelee Island. Troy and Ann Loop — brother Trevor runs the Pelee Island operation — have placed an emphasis on fresh, seasonal, local foods. Accordingly, their menu changes every two months in order to feature the best produce of the moment. Summer will bring dishes featuring Essex County's bountiful tomatoes; fall relies on squashes and other autumnal crops. Year-round, they find something special. Although now only a restaurant, the Loops have plans to expand the Vintage Goose to an inn. If anything like the Tin Goose, it will be a treat.

For more information contact The Convention & Visitors Bureau of Windsor, Essex County & Pelee Island, City Centre Mall, Suite 103, 333 Riverside Drive West, Windsor, Ontario N9A 5K4; 519-255-6530 or 1-800-265-3633.

NATURAL ATTRACTIONS
Port Burwell Provincial Park

On hot summer weekend days, this park just west of Port Burwell is crowded with visitors from the town and other nearby areas who come to enjoy the beach, which is more than a mile

Swimming and fishing from the pier at Rondeau Provincial Park.

long. The other major part of the park is given over to a wooded campground set back from the lake with room for 232 tents or RVs. The Ravine Creek Trail runs west of the camping area; in the summer there are guided nature hikes.

Springtime brings birders to the park to see the exhausted (and therefore quite immobile) migrating birds that have ended their long flight across the lake. Unusual plants can also be found in the park, including adder's tongue fern.

There are picnic areas, a playground, badminton and volleyball nets, and a boat launch nearby. On summer nights, movies are shown in the campground's amphitheater.

For more information contact Port Burwell Provincial Park, PO Box 9, Port Burwell, Ontario N0J 1T0; 519-874-4691.

John E. Pearce Provincial Park

This is an undiscovered secret among the Provincial Parks along

the shore. Tiny John E. Pearce Park near Tyrconnell is for day-use only, and consists of woods high on a bluff overlooking the lake. Its shaded picnic area offers a spectacular view. Because there are no services here, except for rest rooms, at present there is no admission fee. Recently in danger of being closed, the park is now administered by the Tyrconnell Heritage Society as part of a lease agreement on a historical property across the street which is owned by the government.

The home on the property, the Backus-Page House, is being restored by the society. Built in 1850, it is the oldest house in the township. Andrew and Mary Jane Backus (a branch of the Backus family of Port Rowan) raised 12 children in the house, which was in the heart of the Talbot settlement. It's quite likely that Col. Talbot dined in the dining room here. Visitors can tour the house if there's someone on the grounds, even though there is still much restoration work to be done.

Just down the street is St. Peter's Anglican Church, founded in 1827, where services are still held every Sunday, May through October. Across the street, in the cemetery over looking the lake, is Col. Thomas Talbot's grave, marked by a large engraved stone. The cemetery is dedicated to those who risked their lives to settle the north shore of Lake Erie.

For more information contact Port Burwell Provincial Park, PO Box 9, Port Burwell, Ontario N0J 1T0; 519-874-4691(this park does not have its own office), or the Tyrconnell Heritage Society, PO Box 90, Wallacetown, Ontario N0L 2M0.

Rondeau Provincial Park

About midway between Port Stanley and Leamington is a large peninsula that juts into the lake. Its southern tip curves west-ward, toward the shore, almost touching the tip of another, smaller peninsula on which is the small town of Erieau. The large bay created by the peninsula is called Rondeau Bay, named by French explorers Casson and Galinee. From the name "Ronde Eau," or "Round Water," also comes the name of Ontario's second oldest provincial park, established in 1894.

This is one of the larger provincial parks, and also one of the most beautiful. The largest publicly-owned tract of Carolinian forest can be found at Rondeau. Trees unheard of in other parts of Canada grow here, including 100-foot tulip trees, sassafras and sycamores. The forest is getting old, however, and many of the trees are dying. An overpopulation of deer in the park is making it difficult for the forest to regenerate, since the deer eat young tree seedlings.

Rondeau is known for its birding opportunities. Herons, ducks, geese, swans and bitterns can be spotted in the marsh area along the western side of the park. Warblers arrive in the spring, including the colorful prothonotary warbler, whose largest Canadian breeding ground is here. More than a hundred of the 334 bird species recorded at the park have chosen to nest here.

Plant life at the park is also unusually rich. There are 19 species of orchids, as well as wild yam root, yellow mandarin, swamp rose mallow and yellow pond lilies, most of which are considered rare in Canada.

Shortly beyond the park entrance there is a boat launch ramp and a pier from which many people swim, though the beaches on the east side of the park are more appealing. A little farther into the park is a campground with 258 sites, 106 of them with electricity. The main road continues only about three-quarters of the length of the peninsula (but there are two trails that can take you to the end), where it curves around to the east. Follow the signs to the Visitors Center, on a side road close by, where there are displays about the natural history of the park and a small nature store.

Five trails wind throughout the park, though some parts of them are likely to be underwater if the lake level is high. The approximately one-mile Tulip Tree Trail, near the Visitors Center, is the park's only wheelchair accessible trail. The Spice Bush Trail, also about a mile long, is one of the best places to spot birds. The slightly shorter Black Oak Trail leads through a pine-oak forest. Bicycles are not permitted on these trails.

There are two longer trails, however, on which bikes may be

taken, though with their rough surfaces, mountain or hybrid bikes are the preferred choices. The 4.5-mile one way Marsh Trail begins shortly after the park entrance and leads straight out to the tip of the peninsula, passing through the park's extensive marshes. The five-mile South Point Trail begins where the main road curves toward the east and also leads to the end of the peninsula, but through a more remote area of the park. The park roads are also a pleasant place to cycle since they are shaded and smooth surfaced.

Bugs, as well as humans, find Rondeau a particularly nice place to be. Mosquitoes, chiggers and deer flies can all be a problem at times. Adequate clothing, insect repellent and staying on the trails can help prevent problems with these pesky park inhabitants.

For more information contact Rondeau Provincial Park, R.R. 1, Morpeth, Ontario N0P 1X0; 519-674-5405.

Wheatley Provincial Park

Tucked into a curve at the western base of Point Pelee is Wheatley Provincial Park. Its location at the juncture of a creek system and the lake makes it seem almost like two parks in one — the quiet, wooded creekside areas and the sandy lake shore beaches. It was once the location of a settlement called Pegtown, so named, legend has it, because the dwellings were built on stilts or pegs.

The park is used primarily by campers or those who come to enjoy the beach. Canoe rentals make it possible to explore the scenic creeks that flow next to the four campgrounds. There are a total of 210 sites, 52 of them with electricity.

The beach stretches for more than a mile and is particularly attractive. Shaded picnic tables close to the water make it possible for parents to keep a watchful eye on kids slashing in the water close by.

There are two unmarked, unnamed trails in the park, one of

them along a bluff and through a forest on the east side of the park, the other by the creek on the west side. Two footbridges over the creeks are good places for spotting wildlife, such as the painted and snapping turtles that like to sun themselves on logs, or the herons and egrets that frequent the area.

The park has a large population of opossums, which are relatively rare in Canada. Other mammal inhabitants include foxes, raccoons, deer, and the more common squirrels, chipmunks and skunks.

For more information contact Wheatley Provincial Park, PO Box 640, Wheatley, Ontario N0P 2P0; 519-825-4659.

Point Pelee National Park

Point Pelee is the only national park on Lake Erie, either Canadian or American. It is anything but typical of a Canadian national park. One of the smallest in the system at only eight square miles, it is also one of the most heavily used, with an annual half-million visitors. On a point that extends 12 miles into the lake in the western basin near Leamington, the park has an impressive variety of habitats for such a small area. It contains one of the largest marshes left on the lake, as well as forests, open fields and 12.5 miles of sandy beach. It is the southernmost national park in Canada, and visitors are often surprised by the plants found here, such as prickly pear cactus, which are not found elsewhere in Canada. Tucked into a corner of the most populous part of Ontario, the park is a tiny oasis of natural beauty surrounded by farms, towns and cities.

Although not obvious to the casual observer today, Point Pelee has had a long history of human activity. Native people lived on the point from as early as 600 AD. French explorers were the first Europeans to set eyes on Point Pelee in the late 1600s, and a little more than a hundred years later the British declared it a naval reserve in order to preserve its oak and pine forests for ship building.

White settlers came anyway, illegally setting up housekeeping,

The marsh boardwalk at Point Pelee National Park.

farming and fishing. These squatters eventually developed a large fishing industry from what was supposed to be off-limits land. By 1891, 22 such fisheries were operating from the naval reserve. The settlers cleared land, making way for vineyards, orchards and livestock.

Meanwhile, another group was becoming interested in Point Pelee. The Great Lakes Ornithological Club, headed by naturalist W.E. Saunders, was founded to study the bird migration of the Great Lakes area, Point Pelee in particular. They enlisted the help of Jack Miner, already famous for his bird sanctuary nearby, in order to persuade the government to set aside the point as a national park. On May 29, 1918, their wish came true.

This did nothing, however, to lessen human impact on the park. It became an Ontario playground. Cottage developments sprang up, hotels were built, and campers arrived by the droves. In 1963, there were 781,000 visitors to the park, making overwhelming demands on this small and fragile area. The Royal Commission on Government Organization recommended that the park be closed.

Enough people opposed this proposition, however, that a plan was constructed to save the park. The Master Plan for Point Pelee National Park went into effect in 1972. Under the terms of the plan, private land was bought back by the government, houses were removed or destroyed and the park was designated for day-use only, eliminating the camping that had been so damaging. In addition, a public transport system was put into place to take visitors to the tip during peak months so that vehicle traffic could be kept to a minimum.

Today, the only evidence of habitation is on the DeLaurier History Trail, where a 1840s squatter homestead has been reconstructed.

The best place to begin a visit to the park is the Visitor Center, at the southernmost point on the main road. There are exhibits and a 20-minute video that gives background on the natural and human history of the park. The center also distributes visitor guides and interpretive guides and maps for the trails. The Nature Nook Book Store is here, the proceeds of which go to the park programs.

From April through October a free tram service operates between the Visitors Center and the tip area. During other times of the year, private vehicles are permitted. However, anytime of the year it makes a pleasant walk. From the end of the road it's a quarter-mile walk on a trail that leads to an observation platform and the southernmost point of mainland Canada. While it may be tempting to take a dip in the water here, park officials warn that strong currents make it dangerous to do so.

Instead, there are five beach locations elsewhere in the park, all except one with rest rooms, picnic tables, grills and parking. There are no lifeguards.

One of the highlights of Point Pelee is the Marsh Boardwalk, off the main road in the northern section of the park. The boardwalk, approximately a mile long, leads in a loop out over the marsh where an incredible variety of wildlife and plants can be observed. Painted turtles and Blanding's turtles, with their distinguishing yellow throats, can often be seen sunning themselves. Three species of frogs live in the marsh. Though snakes are not very common along the boardwalk, visitors may see a northern watersnake or a rare fox snake, which makes an intimidating sound when frightened, like a rattlesnake, but is completely harmless. Waterfowl are also seen in abundance, along with the scarlet patches of red-winged blackbirds.

Four kinds of water lilies grow in the marsh, as well as the rose mallow, a variety of hibiscus whose delicate pink blossoms can be seen in late July and August. Bladderwort, which lives submerged except for its flowers, is a carnivorous plant that traps small organisms in tiny bladders on its leaves and stems. The marsh is often thick with duckweed, the world's smallest flowering plant that looks, until closer examination, like a green carpet floating on the water.

Perhaps the best way to see Point Pelee's marsh is to rent a canoe at the livery located next to the boardwalk entrance. The park also offers naturalist-led canoe trips through the marsh.

Hikers will find several trails in the park. Tilden's Wood Trail and the Woodland Nature Trail are accessed from the Visitors Center. The DeLaurier Trail begins at the main road about midway in the park. Most trails are wide and paved with gravel, minimizing concern about deer ticks. However, mosquitoes and horse flies can be annoying. The Centennial Biking/Hiking Trail runs parallel to the road for three miles, beginning at the Marsh Boardwalk. Additionally, the park roads are good for cycling. Bike rentals are available at the Marsh Boardwalk.

There are six picnic areas with rest rooms, shelters, tables, and grills. The Blue Heron and White Pine shelters have wood-burning stoves, water and rest rooms that are open all year. The White Pine shelter can be reserved, for a fee. For those who don't think to bring their own food into the park, the Cattail Cafe, near the Marsh Boardwalk, serves carry-out sandwiches, snacks and ice cream.

The park is open year-round, with many visitors coming in the

winter months to enjoy cross-country skiing, hiking and ice skating. The biggest influx of visitors, though comes in the spring along with the birds. As many as 25,000 birders descend on the park each spring to see the hundreds of different species that stop at the point. More than 360 species have been recorded here, making it one of the best places for bird watching in North America. The birds often arrive exhausted from their long trip over the lake, exacerbated at times by cold air or rain. When such a "grounding" takes place literally hundreds of tired birds can be seen on the tip alone.

The fall migration, while not so dramatic, also attracts many visitors. The shape of the peninsula acts as a giant funnel, drawing birds south until they come to the lake. They often congregate on the tip to wait for evening, when they will begin their journey across the water. Monarch butterflies by the thousands also pass through Point Pelee in the fall. They gather at the tip to wait for good crossing conditions, often clumped together on trees and bushes, creating a "butterfly tree."

For more information contact Point Pelee National Park, RR#1, Leamington, Ontario N8H 3V4; 519-322-2365.

Holiday Beach Conservation Area

More than people flock to Holiday Beach Conservation Area on the lake south of Amherstburg. Every fall, September through November, thousands of hawks, eagles, harriers and other birds of prey pass over the park, riding the warm thermal air columns that rise over land to look for the shortest passage across the Detroit River. One record-breaking day saw 86,000 Broad-winged hawks pass over. Other fall visitors include migrating hummingbirds, blue jays, bats, Monarch butterflies and dragonflies. There's a large observation tower from which to view all the excitement.

The park offers programs for the public, including hawk banding demonstrations, raptor identification and photo workshops. These take place on Saturdays and Sundays in September after Labor Day and on Sundays in October.

Costumed guide at Fort Malden, Amherstburg.

Holiday Beach is open all year to accommodate various kinds of activities. Each spring the park's pond is stocked with trout. There's a lake beach as well as picnicking and barbecuing area and a nature trail. Camping is permitted spring through fall. During the winter the park is open to cross-country skiers.

For more information contact the Essex Region Conservation Authority, 360 Fairview Ave. W., Essex, Ontario N8M 1Y6; 519-736-3772 or 519-776-5209.

DIVERSIONS

Sparta

This tiny village a few miles northeast of Port Stanley has its roots in the original settlement of Quakers who came to the area in the early 1800s. Walking around its only intersection is like walking through an outdoor museum. Nearly every building has a historical plaque, including the well-known Sparta House, which was built as a hotel in 1844 and which now serves as a tea room. A gallery featuring the work of Sir Peter Robson, Court Painter by Appointment to the Royal House of Stewart, and antique shops make this a wonderful stop. Just outside the town is Qual du Vin Estate Winery, which produces very good wines from Ontario grapes, including Seyval Blanc, Chardonnay, a Cabernet blend and a very unusual maple dessert wine.

Iona

Northwest of Port Stanley is the small village of Iona, where the Southwold Earthworks are located. The ruins of a village dating from the 1500s, it was once inhabited by as many as 800 Neutral Indians, so named by the European settlers because they refused to take part in the fighting among other area tribes. All that remain are the double earth walls winding around its perimeter, now covered with grass. Plaques placed around the ruins tell what little is known of these extinct people.

St. Thomas

Ever wonder where the word "jumbo" came from — as in

A fox snake along the marsh boardwalk, Point Pelee National Park.

"jumbo shrimp" and "jumbo jet"? You'll find the answer in St. Thomas, about a 15-minute drive north of Port Stanley. Visitors entering the town are greeted by the spectacle of a giant concrete elephant. This is Jumbo, and he has quite a story. In 1861, in Mombassa, Kenya, a young elephant was purchased by a German game collector. Jumbo, as he came to be called, spent some time at the Paris Zoo before being traded to the London Zoo. There he grew to be what is believed to be the largest elephant ever in captivity and endeared himself to the Royal Family as well as to the public. A great outcry resulted when he was sold to P.T. Barnum to be used as part of a circus act. Nothing could be done, however, and Jumbo went on tour. His life ended tragically when he was struck by a train in St. Thomas, Ontario, in 1885. In 1985, the town erected the life-size statue of Jumbo to commemorate the 100th anniversary of his death. Poor Jumbo's skeleton is on display at the New York Museum of Natural History.

Also located in St. Thomas are the Elgin Military Museum, the Elgin County Pioneer Museum and the Elgin County Railway

Museum.

Swain Greenhouses

In the tiny town of Eagle, Swain Greenhouses has four-and-a-half acres of tropical plants and cacti under glass. And smack in the middle of it is the Texas Longhorn Restaurant, a cafeteria-style eatery that features Texas Beef Burgers and Texas Steaks, though there's plenty to eat for those who aren't beef fans. All sandwiches are served on homemade bread, accompanied by hand-cut fries. But the main event here is dessert — every kind of pie you could think of, including the tallest piece of apple pie you've ever seen. If you prefer your sweets in other forms, there's an unbelievable variety of cakes and muffins — all of them made on the premises. Anyone traveling through this part of Ontario shouldn't miss Swain's.

Amherstburg

Though not located on Lake Erie, Amherstburg's strategic location on the Detroit River insured it an important role in Lake Erie history. Originally French, the settlement was one of the first on the lake. In 1760 it came under British ownership. By 1800 it was an important military shipbuilding center. During the War of 1812, the H.M.S. Detroit, the flagship of the British at the Battle of Lake Erie, was built here. Today the old shipyard is the King's Navy Yard Park, a beautiful waterfront park with manicured lawns and flower gardens.

Nearby is Fort Malden National Historic Park. Built by the British in 1796, the fort played an important part in the War of 1812 and later during the Canadian uprising of 1837. After their defeat in the Battle of Lake Erie, the British burned the original fort and the site was occupied by American soldiers. The Americans built the earthworks surrounding the buildings that remain today. No traces of the original fort are left. The fort museum, located in an old laundry and bakery, sheds much light on the military history of the area. There is a self-guided walking tour of the grounds. During the summer there are daily musket firing demonstrations and cooking demonstrations. The fort is open daily May 1 to December 24.

The Gordon House, built in 1798, is run by a private organization working to build a replica of the Detroit. It houses a tea room, marine exhibit and gift shop in the oldest building originally built in Amherstburg.

The oldest building not originally built in the town is now the Historic Park House Museum, just down the street. Built in 1796, the house originally stood in Detroit, which was then British property. The owner, a fierce Loyalist, was dismayed when the Jay Treaty of 1799 ceded Detroit to the Americans. So he moved his house, piece by piece, across the river into British territory.

Before the American Civil War, many escaped slaves sought freedom in Canada by crossing the Detroit River into Amherstburg. At the North American Black Historical Museum and Cultural Centre visitors can learn about the Underground Railroad and the contributions of the first black settlers in Essex County.

For more information about the museums and hours of operation, contact the Amherstburg, Anderdon and MaldenChamber of Commerce, PO Box 24, Amherstburg, Ontario N9V 2Z2; 519-736-2001.

About the author

After many years as a piano teacher, Donna Marchetti now devotes her time to writing and traveling. Her articles have appeared in the *New York Times*, *Los Angeles Times*, Cleveland *Plain Dealer*, Rodale's *Scuba Diving* and many other publications in the U.S. and abroad. When not roaming the shores of Lake Erie, she makes every excuse to traipse through the Caribbean and Micronesia, about which she has written extensively.

Donna lives with her husband and son in Cleveland, Ohio, where she enjoys scuba diving, cycling and reading. She has, over the past two years of researching this book, developed an unparalleled affection for Lake Erie perch and Lake Erie wines.

THE BEST OF LAKE ERIE

Dealing in superlatives is always risky business. What seems exceptional to one may be only ordinary to another, and vice versa. Nonetheless, here is a list — albeit a highly subjective one — of some of the lake's best offerings.

Best Beaches
Crane Creek State Park, Ohio
Headlands State Park, Ohio
Point Pelee National Park, Ontario
Presque Isle State Park, Pa.

Most Fun for Kids
Geneva-on-the-Lake, Ohio
Port Dover, Ontario
Put-in-Bay, Ohio

Most Fun for Adults
Port Stanley, Ontario
Put-in-Bay, Ohio
Vermilion, Ohio

Best Restaurants
Chez Francois, Vermilion, Ohio
Kettle Creek Inn, Port Stanley, Ontario
William Seward Inn, Westfield, N.Y.

Best Lake Erie Perch
Brennan's Fish House, Grand River, Ohio

Best Lake Erie Walleye (Pickerel)
The Island Restaurant (at the Anchor and Wheel), Pelee Island, Ontario

Best Natural Attractions
Point Pelee National Park, Ontario
Presque Isle State Park, Pa.

Best Museums and Historical Sites
Fort Erie, Ontario

Best B&B (Expensive)
Water's Edge Retreat, Kelleys Island, Ohio

Best B&Bs (Moderate)
Captain Montague's, Huron, Ohio
Five Bells Inn, Port Clinton, Ohio

Best Inns
Kettle Creek Inn, Port Stanley, Ontario
William Seward Inn, Westfield, N.Y.

Best Shopping
Port Stanley, Ontario (clothing, gifts)
Vermilion, Ohio (gifts)
Westfield, N.Y. (antiques)

Best Wineries
Firelands Winery, Sandusky, Ohio
Markko Vineyards, Conneaut, Ohio
Pelee Island Winery, Pelee Island and Kingsville, Ontario
Presque Isle Wine Cellars, North East, Pa.